ACTIVE LEARNING
Games to Enhance Academic Abilities

ACTIVE LEARNING

Games to Enhance Academic Abilities

BRYANT J. CRATTY

University of California, Los Angeles

PRENTICE-HALL, INC., *Englewood Cliffs, New Jersey*

ACTIVE LEARNING
Bryant J. Cratty   Games to Enhance Academic Abilities

© 1971   by Prentice-Hall, Inc., Englewood Cliffs, New Jersey

P   13–003491–6
C   13–003509–2

Library of Congress Catalog Number 78–181360

Printed in the United States of America

Current printing (last digit)
10 9 8 7 6 5 4

London   Prentice-Hall International, Inc.
Sydney   Prentice-Hall of Australia, Pty. Ltd.
Toronto   Prentice-Hall of Canada, Ltd.
New Delhi   Prentice-Hall of India Private Limited
Tokyo   Prentice-Hall of Japan, Inc.

Preface

This text was written with two main objectives in mind: First, to explain in the simplest terms just how various active games may be employed to enhance various academic skills; Second, as reflected in the final chapter to present a survey of methods for dealing with coordination problems.

The games were devised partly as the result of research carried out within the Catholic Archdiocese in the City of Los Angeles during the 1968–69, the 1969–70, and the 1970–71 school years. I am grateful to Father Mihan, Sister Carol Ann, and to the members of his staff as well as to the principals and faculty members of the 15 schools who were involved in the investigation during these years. My thanks are also extended to the charming children who seemed to be happy and productive while playing the games we presented to them.

These games and activities may be used in many ways: as occasional activities in elementary school programs to provide youngsters with motivation, or as a central core for the instruction of immature normal youngsters or retarded children. Both uses have been employed by various schools in Los Angeles and in other parts of the country. Some of the activities should be applied selectively. The games are accompanied by paragraphs describing what kinds of children are most likely to benefit. Modifications of many of the games permit their use with physically-handicapped youngsters, while the large configurations used in most of the games are helpful to children with visual problems.

Sister Margaret Mary Martin of my staff coordinated the program during these years, and to her go my heartfelt thanks. She worked with great energy and dedication during the past three years, while on leave from Alverno College in Milwaukee, Wisconsin, where she is Chairman of the Physical Education Department. The instructors on my staff, Mrs. Jane Durkin, Misses Marilyn Cohen, Dianne Jue, and Susan Brinn, were also vital to the success of this program.

My secretarial staff, composed of Misses Sara Dobbins, Barbara Goen and Loralyn Godby, edited and polished the final manuscript. Without their help and that of others in a similar role during the past several years, I would have been far less productive.

B. J. C.

Contents

1   Introduction   **Chapter 1**
    10   Summary
    11   Bibliography

13   Calming Down and Tuning Up   **Chapter 2**
    25   Bibliography

26   Geometric Figures   **Chapter 3**
    36   Summary
    36   Bibliography

37   Remembering Things   **Chapter 4**
    46   Summary

47   Numbers and Counting   **Chapter 5**
    59   Summary

viii

Contents

Chapter 6   Mathematics   60
     Summary   *77*

Chapter 7   Letters   78
     Summary   *90*

Chapter 8   Letter Sounds and Spelling   91
     Summary   *103*

Chapter 9   Reading   104
     Summary   *116*

Chapter 10   How, To Whom, With What, How Often, and Why?   118
     Summary   *131*
     Bibliography   *131*

Chapter 11   Improving Coordination   132
     Summary   *156*
     Bibliography   *157*
     Equipment   *157*

Games

Chapter 2

19   *Game 1*   Tighten and Relax

20   *Game 2*   Head to Toe and Back Again

20   *Game 3*   How Slowly Can You . . . ?

21   *Game 4*   Don't Drop It!

21   *Game 5*   Me and My Shadow

22   *Game 6*   Fast and Slow

Chapter 3

28   *Game 7*   See and Match

29   *Game 8*   Jump and Say

29   *Game 9*   Hear and Jump

30   *Game 10*   See and Throw

30   *Game 11*   Go and Get It

31   *Game 12*   Cut and Find

31   *Game 13*   Big Things and Little Things

32   *Game 14*   Jump and Tape

33   *Game 15*   Find It In the Maze

34   *Game 16*   Find It and Do It, In Order

Left Things and Right Things   *Game 17*   35
Lots of Things   *Game 18*   35

Chapter 4   Where Did I Visit?   *Game 19*   39
Repeat Myself   *Game 20*   40
Tell Me Where I Went   *Game 21*   41
Tell Me What I Did   *Game 22*   42
Ball Things   *Game 23*   42
Add One   *Game 24*   43
Left and Right   *Game 25*   44
Arrange and Show   *Game 26*   45
Many Things   *Game 27*   45
Many Things At Many Places   *Game 28*   46

Chapter 5   Look and Match   *Game 29*   48
Hear, Say, and Jump   *Game 30*   49
Drawing, Touching, and Jumping   *Game 31*   50
Run Through It   *Game 32*   50
More Numbers, Many Digits   *Game 33*   52
Running In the Sand   *Game 34*   52
Spaceship   *Game 35*   52
Counting Relays   *Game 36*   54
Run and Jump, Counting Relays   *Game 37*   55
Jump and Count   *Game 38*   55
See Quick and Hop   *Game 39*   55
Partner Write and Tell   *Game 40*   56
How Many Can You?   *Game 41*   57
How Many Did I?   *Game 42*   58
How Far Can You Jump?   *Game 43*   58

Chapter 6   Find the Sign   *Game 44*   61
Collect and Count   *Game 45*   62
Take Away the Squares   *Game 46*   63
Jump the Answer   *Game 47*   63
Hop the Problems   *Game 48*   64
Jump and Reach   *Game 49*   65
Addition Relays   *Game 50*   66
Subtraction Runs   *Game 51*   67
Take Away Broadjumps   *Game 52*   68
Throwing Best Subtraction   *Game 53*   69
Decimal Races   *Game 54*   70
Team Base Count and Add   *Game 55*   70
Time-Tables Leap   *Game 56*   71
Hear and Hop   *Game 57*   72

73   Game 58   Answer Running
74   Game 59   Progressive Addition
74   Game 60   Problems and Answers
75   Game 61   Percentage Basketball
75   Game 62   Track Division
76   Game 63   Finding Out About Football

81   Game 64   Match and Jump
82   Game 65   Tell, Find, and Tell
82   Game 66   Find Them
83   Game 67   The Sandbox
84   Game 68   Playground Letters
84   Game 69   Alphabet Games
85   Game 70   Letter Hopscotch
87   Game 71   Letter Relays
88   Game 72   Cutting, Looking, and Finding
88   Game 73   Flash and Jump
88   Game 74   Upper-Case, Lower-Case
90   Game 75   Script, Printing

94   Game 76   Shown and Sound
94   Game 77   Vowel Sounds
95   Game 78   Consonant Sounds
96   Game 79   Spelling: See, Hear, and Spell
96   Game 80   Anagrams
97   Game 81   Team Spelling
97   Game 82   Spelling Relays
98   Game 83   Running Spelling Games
99   Game 84   Hear and Spell
99   Game 85   Hearing and Spelling Relays
100   Game 86   Spell a Story
100   Game 87   Same or Opposite
100   Game 88   Spell It and Do It
101   Game 89   The Same But Different
101   Game 90   Definitions
102   Game 91   Writing and Printing
103   Game 92   Musical Letters

106   Game 93   See and Jump
107   Game 94   Draw and Hop
108   Game 95   Hop and Say
108   Game 96   Steal the Word
109   Game 97   Story Relays
109   Game 98   Read and Act

Chapter 7

Chapter 8

Chapter 9

Reading Directions   *Game 99*   *110*
Matching Words   *Game 100*   *111*
Base Progress   *Game 101*   *111*
Reading Basketball   *Game 102*   *112*
Read, Pass, or Throw   *Game 103*   *113*
Obstacle Course Reading   *Game 104*   *114*
Write a Story   *Game 105*   *115*
Wait and Read   *Game 106*   *115*
Read and Run   *Game 107*   *116*

Chapter 11   Jumping Things   *Game 108*   *150*
Tumbling Things   *Game 109*   *151*
Balance Things   *Game 110*   *151*
Throwing, Catching, and
Hitting Balls   *Game 111*   *152*

ACTIVE LEARNING
Games to Enhance Academic Abilities

Chapter 1

Introduction

This book is about physical activity but not about physical education or athletics. It is about how children can learn, but it is not about classroom teaching techniques. It indicates how learning can be made a happy experience by including in the process various games and physical activities. It illustrates fun-filled techniques for teaching basic academic operations that have formerly been pounded into children's psyches in less than happy ways.

This approach is not entirely new; neither does it represent some kind of educational cure-all. Educators, parents, and teachers are constantly deluged with learning panaceas. Educational overkill in the form of expansive and unsupported claims for new educational practices may be as destructive to the curriculum as certain kinds of military overkill techniques may be to mankind. The new ways of teaching described in this book will not replace other, more traditional methods, but should make learning more palatable and effective.

The general approach outlined here was originally spawned several centuries ago. Educators in France and Germany in the late 1700s and early 1800s observed that children are active beings who become joyful when they are permitted to move freely. These educators believed that children *need* movement: if the need is stifled, children will likely perform less capably in a variety of traditional learning tasks. As a result of these insights, unstructured and structured play experiences were introduced into some schools.

These educational philosophers of two and three centuries ago viewed activity much as do many current educators. They seemed to say, when constructing their programs, that movement should be introduced in the schools for two main reasons: (1) to produce more relaxed and joyful children, who would then be more willing learners within the laborious classroom, and (2) to release children's tensions that might inhibit their efforts to learn "more important" subjects than would be found on the playfield, gymnasia, and grassy knolls. In this text bodily movement is viewed not as a way to reduce unpleasant overtones of classroom learning but as a method incorporated directly into the learning of academic operations usually taught in a restrictive classroom environment.

Activity in Class

Anyone who has watched children and has observed schools in session has probably concluded that children, particularly younger children, like to move, but that in many classrooms relatively little movement is tolerated. Good, capable children are usually those viewed by their teachers as children who pay attention, sit still, cooperate, and otherwise maintain immobile postures during the time they are actually involved in the learning processes.

Research data collected over the last forty years indicate that immobility may not ensure optimum intellectual learning. For example, American researchers in the 1930s found that subjects could memorize better when they exerted about half their effort on a hand grip. In the 1950s another investigator found that reasonably fit people, given moderate exercise, performed better in mathematical tasks. In the 1960s a Swedish scholar found that a subject walking on a treadmill at about 50 percent of his maximum speed performed better at arithmetic problems (heard via earphones while he walked) than he did when he was standing still or running at a fast speed.

In the late 1960s, Norwegian psychologists found that, if fit, activity-oriented children who were confined for prolonged periods of time began to perform progressively more poorly on tests of intelligence. In this same experiment the less fit, relatively passive children continued to perform up to their capabilities, even after six hours of a program that included two IQ tests and two hours of intensive study.

Scholars have concluded that there are children of various learning types. Some learn best by passively taking in what is presented to them by their teachers; others learn best by doing and being physically active when they learn. Furthermore, it seems that healthy children with high activity needs become increasingly inhibited in the effort they bring to intellectual efforts the longer they are confined to a classroom. These active children are not dumb and do not become dumb when sitting; they just become unable to apply appropriate effort in passive situations when their personalities and needs literally cry for movement.

Too Much Activity

There are groups of children who, particularly within recent years, have attracted the attention of physicians, psychologists, and educators. These are the children who are *too active* most of the time at home, in classrooms, or wherever they happen to alight momentarily. These children are said to be hyperactive. They move too much and in inappropriate ways; they leave their seats too often to please the teacher; when they are in their seats, they often keep their eyes and hands busy in tasks not related to what is happening in the classroom.

Several approaches have been used on these children, and some of them have been helpful. Often the children are placed on medication that tends to slow down their activity but does not dull them intellectually. At times the children are placed in (or may choose to go into) small office-like cubicles where they can concentrate on their schoolwork without distraction. Relaxation exercises and practice in slow motions have also helped to curb hyperactivity.

Probably some of these active children (usually boys) were not always much more active than many of their fellow students. However, their active behavior may have been punished inordinately by teachers or may have attracted the censure of parents and other authority figures. This adult punishment, instead of calming them down, had the reverse effect. Some became mildly emotionally disturbed, as reflected in increased levels of activity. Hyperactivity may also be a way for some children to block out disturbing demands made on them by adults who seek to control them excessively.

Although it is certainly necessary to help such children to calm down, at the same time it seems possible to adjust the school curriculum in part, so that it matches more closely some of the movement needs of some of the children participating.

The activities in this text provide content for this type of active curriculum; a course of study that recognizes the behavioral tendencies of more types of children may result in fewer failures during the early elementary school years.

Clumsy Children

There are subtle ways in which children's movements interact with their total performance at school. During recent years various professional groups have focused attention on "clumsy" children. Children possessing coordination problems are said to evidence the "clumsy child syndrome." Psychologists and educators have often noticed that clumsiness is more often seen among children with learning difficulties than among children who read, write, and otherwise conduct themselves well in classrooms.

Some have speculated that relieving children of their clumsiness with various kinds of training techniques may remediate learning problems and enhance the classroom functioning of normal children. Careful research on this problem, however, has revealed that there are no short-cuts to spelling and reading that may be taken by walking balance beams.

However, a child who cannot perform well physically often experiences a number of problems that affect his classroom performance directly, while other by-products of clumsiness negatively influence learning in more subtle ways . For example, when clumsiness is reflected in poor handwriting or printing, a child experiences extreme psychological discomfort in a classroom. Despite the fact that he may be basically intelligent, he cannot translate his thoughts to the page in front of him in the allotted time. He is likely to experience extreme frustration and may refuse to start his lessons because he knows he may later be punished for not finishing them on time. He may know the answer to a series of mathematics problems but be unable to write the answers down fast enough on an arithmetic test. His writing assignments are labored, difficult to read, and traumatic for teachers, parents, and himself.

There are numerous indirect ways in which clumsiness in children may reflect in their classroom functioning.[1] My colleagues and I have found that, almost without exception, clumsy boys report that their friends make fun of them, that other boys dislike them, that they are the last to be chosen in games, and that they watch instead of play. Although not usually admitting that they feel clumsy, in tests we have given them they invariably report that they experience a good deal of social punishment at play meted out by their peers. It is a likely assumption that the unhappiness these children feel on the playground often reflects on their schoolwork when they return to the classroom after recess or physical education.

Another interesting finding has emerged from studies with clumsy boys. When we ask these boys what games they

---

[1] The estimates by experts concerning the incidence of this type of mild to moderate coordination problem in groups of otherwise normal children have run from 10–30 percent. Most feel that from 15–18 percent of all children in the elementary and secondary schools suffer from some kind of measurable coordination problem.

like to play, their answers reveal that to a marked degree their game choices are identical with girls of the same age. It appears that clumsy boys are "kicked out" of the more physically demanding boys' games and either do not play at all or gravitate toward the hopscotch court or jump-rope area inhabited by their feminine classmates. It is well known that both adults and children generally adopt behavioral characteristics of people with whom they associate for prolonged periods of time. Thus it might be assumed that in some cases these clumsy boys, after playing with the girls, may adopt feminine gestures and facial mannerisms that are likely to lead to further social ostracism.

Girls, too, need a reasonable level of competency in games and other activities to be socially acceptable. Bicycle riding, skating, and dancing are highly prized activities in which girls in childhood and adolescence should participate for maximum social development.

Communication includes movements and verbal behavior. Gestures, bodily posturings, and facial expressions add depth to words transmitted from child to child or from child to adult. Clumsy children may experience difficulty in communication because of the inability to manage their movements efficiently.

A few years ago a group of psychiatrists in Texas studied what they termed "bumping" behavior in children. This study involved scoring the number of times various children contacted—that is, bumped—their fellow classmates while moving around the schoolroom, walking through the halls, and running around the playground. The researchers were surprised to find that a small group of clumsy children contacted their fellows to a far greater degree than did the majority of those who moved normally. Furthermore, these frequent contacts were likely to elicit hostility from those who were bumped. It became clear, after more extensive observations, that indeed these clumsy bumping children could not help themselves. They could not refrain from jostling their classmates because they carried with them perceptual problems relative to space. They seemed unable to determine how much room there was between Johnny and the desk for them to pass through. Their clumsiness contributed to the inaccuracy with which they moved among their friends.

This book was written for both teachers and parents, for often a child with learning difficulties can be helped by those at home who take an interest in him. Too often, however, parents' attempts to aid him resemble the methods used by his teachers—methods he has rejected or shrugged off.

Parents of preschool children may also find some of the information and games outlined in this book helpful when evaluating their child's readiness for school and as they prepare him to meet the demands of the first grade. Generally, children from reasonably privileged environments enter the first grade able to block-print their first name and to identify many, if not most, letters of the alphabet. The games in Chapters 7 and 8 should contribute to the early development of these operations in the preschooler. It is not our intent to cram knowledge in the preschooler before he is ready; at the same time most parents want to know that their child is starting off at least even with others he will compete with during his first year in school.

Atypical Children

Many of the sequences, techniques, and games here described have been employed for several years by teachers dealing with retarded and/or physically handicapped children and youth. The child of seven who is labeled an educable retardate functions intellectually like a normal five-year-old and thus can take advantage of games intended to teach letter and pattern recognition, spelling, and similar operations.

The teen-age retardate with an IQ of from 30–50 (usually labeled a "trainable") similarly has been shown to progress when exposed to many of the activities outlined in the following chapters. In addition, many retarded children evidence coordination problems, so that learning techniques that incorporate total body movement are likely to improve both the academic competencies inherent in the games and the movement qualities needed to carry them out.

Many of the games are easily adaptable for children with various physical handicaps. A child in a wheelchair, for example, may throw a bean bag into a square containing a letter, rather than hop or jump there like his more capable classmate. The result is the same—an enjoyable way to learn letters, words, numbers, counting, and even reading.

Research

Sophisticated school administrators, curriculum supervisors, teachers, and parents are asking themselves whether the new methods of teaching classroom skills really are more helpful than the more traditional approaches. This questioning is a healthy sign, I believe, for too often educational practices that have been less than sound have been incorporated too rapidly into the school curriculum without the necessary verification in the form of valid research findings. The concept of educational overkill was previously alluded to in this chapter.

Particular skepticism should be directed toward any technique—whether balance-beam walking, visual training, or crawling on the floor—that is vastly different from the classroom operation it is purported to remediate. Generally, the proponents of these types of extraclassroom techniques state rather emphatically that their methods will indeed "transfer" in rather direct ways back into the classroom and aid a variety of educational, intellectual, and perceptual problems of children.[2]

If a technique unlike spelling is engaged in to purportedly help spelling, there should be sufficient proof of two things: (1) that taking a diverse course to teach spelling is more helpful than teaching spelling in the direct ways now usually employed, and (2) that indeed the unusual remedial techniques employed will truly transfer in a direct way to spelling.

With regard to the games, techniques, and approaches

---

[2] I have written a number of texts examining the worth of these practices in the sometimes "hard light" of the available research evidence. See References 3 and 5 at the end of this chapter.

that follow, several statements may be made. (1) A reasonable amount of research was carried out during the years 1967–1971 that produced findings supporting the worth of many of the techniques. Some of these data will be alluded to in various parts of the text. (The diligent reader who wants to evaluate the original drafts of this research can do so by consulting the bibliographies at the ends of the various chapters in this book.) (2) Many of the techniques employed do not need proof that they somehow transfer to classroom operations; indeed they *are* these same operations simply conducted in a different form. Jumping in a grid and spelling is spelling; reading a word instructing a child to execute a movement is reading! Legitimate criticism and healthy skepticism, however, should be directed toward literal application of these techniques to large groups of intellectually capable children in middle and late childhood. This book does not represent the answer to the multitude of complex learning problems encountered by the numerous types of children presently occupying our schools. Rather it is hoped that discerning teachers, parents, and curriculum specialists will come away with another helpful set of tools with which to sharpen the minds of the nation's children and youth.

The Games Children Play

There are several other interesting relationships among fitness, games children play, and intelligence that justify the use of learning games in elementary and secondary schools. For example, one authority has recently stated that, to an increased degree, American children are choosing to play games combining the use of intelligence and strategy. This is to be expected, because the young of all civilizations generally incorporate into their games the skills they perceive as important in adulthood. The aborigine child becomes adroit at catching small game with his father's snares, and the American child seems to be preparing himself for tasks he thinks he will later need for success as an adult.

If left to their own devices, it is probable that American children will choose games requiring less and less vigorous activity, despite the fact that they still have basic physical fitness needs that should be met. A recent study in Norway underlined this same trend. It was found that in early childhood the more fit children seemed to be the less capable scholars, whereas the less fit children learned to read first and spent more time in their books during the first years of elementary school. The second finding of this interesting study was that in *later* childhood years the more fit children were the *best* scholars. The researchers hypothesized that, as games became more complex in late childhood, incorporating challenging strategies and rules, more intelligent children began to play them. And this increased interest plus participation resulted in higher correlations between academic ability and physical vigor in late childhood than was seen in earlier childhood.

Data of this nature suggest that, unless childhood games are made intellectually challenging, there may be a division created between children who play and become fit versus those who withdraw from activity and exercise their intellects in passive ways. Problems of this nature, while needing further research, at the same time have produced data that support the inclusion of vigorous learning games into the schools—games combining the opportunity to gain fitness with the opportunity to learn academic skills and exercise intellectual capacities.

Summary

Movement games may help the child with learning problems, may aid the active normal child to learn better, and may improve the academic progress of the culturally deprived and retarded child.

Activity and academic learning interact in several obvious and subtle ways. Too much activity or too much passivity may impede learning in children, just as will the restraining of active, fit children too long in classrooms. Curricula may be adjusted to better meet the needs of both the active and the more passive children they now serve. The games in the following chapters contain methods in which a more active curriculum may be devised.

Clumsiness in children can have emotional overtones that may negatively affect learning. Children who do not play games well report receiving an inordinate amount of social punishment from their classmates, and this censure in turn is likely to lead to a low self-concept and academic functioning that is less than optimum.

Additionally, poor hand-eye coordination is usually manifested in less than adequate efforts to print and write letters and words. The last chapter in this text contains helpful ways of remediating coordination problems in a child who cannot keep up with his friends in their games, as well as those who cannot write well in the classroom.

Bibliography

CRATTY, B. J., *Perceptual-Motor Behavior and Educational Processes.* Springfield, Ill.: Charles C. Thomas, Publisher, 1968.
This text contains surveys and essays evaluating current practices involving perceptual-motor education as related to classroom performance.

———, *Motor Activity and the Education of Retardates.* Philadelphia: Lea & Febiger, Publishers, 1969.
The content of this text is similar to that of *Perceptual-Motor Efficiency in Children*, but theory sections are directed toward the problems of the retarded and the remediation of coordination difficulties in retarded children.

———, *Educational Implications of Movement Experiences.* Seattle, Wash.: Special Child Publications, 1970.
This publication evaluates the research dealing with perceptual-motor education relative to the improvement of reading.

———, and SISTER M. M. MARTIN, *The Effects of Learning Games upon Children with Learning Difficulties.* Los Angeles: Department of Physical Education, University of California at Los Angeles, Monograph 1971.

———, and SISTER M. M. MARTIN, *Perceptual-Motor Efficiency in Children.* Philadelphia: Lea & Febiger, 1969.
This book contains a number of techniques, evaluation procedures, etc., for the identification and remediation of movement problems in children, including handwriting and control of the larger muscles as well as general control of

behavior. Chapters also deal with norms for coordination tests, rhythm, and the self-concept as well as with principles for perceptual-motor training.

———, SISTER M. M. MARTIN, CLAIRE JENNETT, NAMIKO IKEDA, and MARGARET MORRIS, "The Use of Total Body Movement as a Learning Modality" in *Movement Activities, Motor Ability, and the Education of Children.* Springfield, Ill.: Charles C. Thomas, Publishers, 1970.

Chapter **2**

Calming Down and
Tuning Up

There are some children in classrooms who are habitually too excited to work effectively. They move too much with their bodies, and when apparently fixed in their seats, may use their eyes to look at everything but their schoolwork.

The causes for this hyperactive behavior are not always easily detectable, even by professionals. Such a child may simply be immature and, like a younger child, need to physically explore the world around him to a greater degree than would be expected of a child his age. On the other hand, he may be perceptually confused; his visual apparatus may not organize the world effectively, and he may need to thus confirm where things are, how far away they are, and what shape objects take by actually going places and touching things. Sometimes there are slight problems in the complex mechanisms of the brain that control general bodily arousal and activity level. Or the

13

child may have emotional problems that prevent him from concentrating for prolonged periods of time.

Despite differences of opinion concerning just why some children are too active for their own good, there is almost unanimous opinion that an inordinate amount of activity is likely to cause learning difficulties within most educational settings. A variety of methods have been devised to aid such children to become self-controlled and better organized so that they can function well intellectually, emotionally, and socially.

In contrast to the child who moves too much and seems almost too alert is the child who seems habitually sleepy. He is lethargic, hard to interest, and difficult to alert to physical as well as intellectual tasks. He is a dreamer who seems to dream too much, at inappropriate times, and in inappropriate places. Both the active and lethargic child need to be aided to better match their levels of arousal to the tasks they find themselves confronted with in their schools.

Do Children "Wear Out" in Sports?

Among the ways to reduce activity levels in children is to somehow drain off excess energy by requiring them, or motivating them, to engage in a great deal of physical effort. At times, this "drainage theory" does not work very well; often children who have been exposed to this approach become so "high" that they have problems sleeping the night following the vigorous activity, rather than becoming relaxed as would be expected. Physical educators, either through choice or incidentally, are responsible for stimulating children in their games to levels too high for the classroom situation to which they usually return immediately following recess or physical education classes. High levels of activity and physiological arousal are required for games and, indeed, hyperactive children can sometimes (if their other problems are not too great) play reasonably well; however, due to defective mechanisms in the brain, they then may be unable to calm themselves down after vigorous games, unlike the normal child. They are likely to prove almost impossible to the classroom teacher after physical education classes or to their parents on returning home in the evening.

Another more helpful ploy often used in classrooms, and one that can be employed more widely at home, involves creating a small "office" or carrel for the child to study in. Plywood partitions placed on three sides of a small desk will cut off distracting objects and people while the child attempts to do his work. I have observed this practice used in many effective ways. For example, one teacher built two small offices of this nature at the rear of her room, and children who found themselves too overaroused to work could *choose* to go there. The fact that children in this class would frequently evidence this choice implies that indeed children who are too active *do not like to be this way.* Their own behavior upsets them, and, when given one or several methods to relieve their upset condition, they may eagerly take advantage of them.

Medication

When a child is extremely distractible it is often necessary to administer medication that may calm him and enable him and his parents and teachers to work in harmony toward common goals. Physicians (usually pediatricians or pediatric neurologists) who prescribe such drugs generally must try several types and/or dosages as each child's system reacts differently to various ones. After this is carried out, there should be frequent conferences among doctor, parent, and teacher as the child's behavioral changes are observed and accommodated to. It is often possible to calm a child down with medications and also to slow down or remove his extraneous movements while not appreciably dulling his intellectual alertness. In a similar manner, it is often possible to improve a child's coordination and to lengthen his attention span.

A child may be kept on this type of medication for one or more years. An effort is often made to gradually reduce the dosage after six months to a year have passed. As in the use of a closed study space, children are often consciously grateful for the manner in which medication has slowed them down and enabled them to gain heightened self-control, which in turn aids them to function more effectively in a wide variety of social and academic environments.

Calming Down and
Tuning Up

During the past thirty years, several physicians, educators, and psychologists have advanced various techniques, in addition to the ones outlined previously, with which to reduce extraneous and disruptive activity in children. One of the first of these writings appeared in a book titled *Progressive Relaxation*, printed in 1938 and written by Edmund Jacobson, a physician. The German psychiatrist Johannes Schultz published similar techniques in the 1950s.

Research studies in our laboratory have experimented with modifications of the relaxation-training techniques advocated by Jacobson and Schultz and in addition have explored two other ways of encouraging children to gain better control of their movements. Research substantiating the worth of these techniques has appeared in literature emanating from Czechoslovakia as well as in published writings in the United States.

The measures of movement found to correlate highest with academic performance and IQ are those in which normal children are asked to move as slowly as they can in various tasks. The slower a child is willing to move, the more likely it is that he will perform well academically. In a recent investigation, we intercorrelated a number of scores in nineteen mental and motor tests collected from more than 150 children verifying this relationship.

Three "clusters" of scores emerged: one group that correlated highly were the scores from two IQ tests; a second that indicated a close interrelation with each other was a group of scores from various movement tasks involving agility and balance; the third group of scores that "hung together" and that did not correlate with the other two clusters was composed of scores obtained from tasks involving spelling, letter recognition, pattern recognition, and from a task in which children were asked to walk as slowly as they could along a twelve-foot line. The score from this latter test was related to a general classroom operations factor.

In a third research investigation, marked age differences were discovered using various measures of "how slowly can you move?" For example, four-year-olds walked a twelve-foot line in about thirteen seconds and six-year-olds in about thirty-six seconds; the average time for nine-year-olds was almost a minute. Most important, it was found that children who were given such measures just after physical education activities tended to move about twice as fast as when they came from a classroom to be tested in line drawing ("as slowly as you can"). On the other hand, various tasks involving the larger muscles (getting up, walking a twelve-foot-long line) when administered after recess were executed more slowly than when given just after classroom work. It thus appeared that while fatigue of the larger muscles might slow children down and encourage them to sit in their seats more readily after physical education or recess, they remained aroused and this arousal diminished their fine motor skills needed in class. The findings of this same investigation indicated that the measure most predictive of teachers' ratings of children's self-control in class was one in which they were asked to draw a three-foot-long line on a blackboard as slowly as they could.

In a third study, we found that after a period of weeks, we could elicit significant changes in these types of control measures ("how slowly will you walk a line?") and that this improvement was accompanied by improvement in a variety of classroom skills including spelling, letter recognition, and serial memory ability.

Investigations in Czechoslovakia have also indicated that training hyperactive children to relax using the Schultz method, with modifications, resulted in significant changes in various academic tasks. I believe, therefore, that there are sound data supporting the worth of some of the games outlined on the pages in this chapter. If these are applied correctly, they should aid the behavioral control of children who find themselves moving too rapidly, too much, and too often.

Relaxation Training

The overall purpose of this type of training is to give a child an awareness of the extra muscular tension he carries with him. When he becomes aware of this tension, it is then hoped that he will learn to control it, thus reducing hyperactivity that may accompany excess muscle tonus. Although it can be argued, with some validity, that muscular tension is not always accompanied by emotional upset, it is usually found that internal emotional states and outside muscular tension are more intimately connected in children than in adults. Particularly in younger boys, the association between muscle and emotion is an intimate one.

The children in these games should be placed in a comfortable position and verbally instructed to tighten and to relax various muscle groups to varying degrees. The training might start with Game 1, in which the children try to tighten all their muscles and to alternate these contractions with periods of complete relaxation accompanied by slow, deep breathing. Following this, the training might then be continued by concentrating on various muscle groups, as indicated in Game 2.

This type of training should not be continued until the child is excessively fatigued; sessions should last at least three to four minutes and, after some practice, as long as five to ten minutes. This training should be engaged in at any time it is needed—following a family quarrel or when the child is too "high" in a classroom. More able children can often learn to administer it to themselves after a period of time with good results.[1]

The instructions to a child during this training depend to a large degree on the age and sophistication of the child himself. Older children can be given the scientific names of specific muscle groups they are attempting to tighten and relax, whereas younger children must be encouraged to the same ends by using various types of verbal imagery ("Sink deep into the mat," "Make your muscles soft as cotton").

Often this type of relaxation training is used in conjunction with the administration of the medication previously discussed. This training in turn leads to the games in the second section of this chapter.

---

[1]A child in our program at UCLA who recently lost his father is able to apply this training to himself as his tensions mount. A competitive pole-vaulter with whom I am acquainted said that he could relax himself using this method to the extent that he was able to fall asleep between vaults in the US–USSR track meet a few years ago!

Equipment: Mats, chairs.

Method: Have children either lie down or sit in comfortable positions and then have them alternately tighten and relax their total bodies ("Tighten as hard as you can . . . everything . . . tighter.") The tightening phase should last from three to six seconds and be followed by instructions to relax completely or some instructions compatible with the children's levels of understanding ("Become a cloud," "Take the bones out of your muscles"). After several of these contractions the children should be asked to tighten one-half as hard as they can; after a few times, half as hard as that (one-fourth as hard as maximum). All tightening phases should be interspersed with relaxed and deep breathing ("Take a deep breath and let it out completely").

Modifications: Children can be in seated positions, heads on desks, lying on mats. Children can have padding placed under the knees to induce relaxed slight flexion at knees; pillows under head. Duration of time may vary from a few minutes to from five to ten minutes, depending on the ages and mental ability of the children. The words used can vary according to the same criterion.

For: Hyperactive children of all ages and mental abilities.

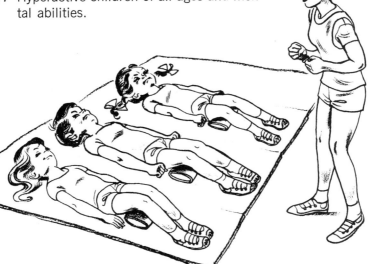

Game 2
Head
to
Toe
and
Back
Again

Equipment: Mats, pads for comfort.
Method: Start with the top of the body and ask children to tighten face, then relax; then neck, shoulders, arms, hips, on down the body; alternate with periods of relaxation and deep breathing. Then up the body again: feet, hips, arms. This may be repeated several times up and down.
Modifications: Concentrate on specific muscle groups within body parts—that is, fists or upper arms. Experiment with partial contractions (one-half, one-fourth) after full contraction and reasonably complete relaxation are achieved. This technique may be used in conjunction with or after Game 1 in this series.
For: Hyperactive children of all ages.

Slow Controlled Movement

During the end of a session of relaxation training, it is often helpful to encourage children not simply to tighten muscles in an immobile fashion, but to move in slow, controlled ways.

Game 3
How
Slowly
Can
You...?

Equipment: Blackboard, mats, tape for making lines.
Method: One or more children can see how slowly they can move in various ways ("Draw a line as slowly as you can," "Get up from the mat as slowly as you can," "Walk a line as slowly as you can"). Clock time and give child evidence of improvement. Charts may be made showing improvement.
Modifications: More than one child can compete in one task at a time. Competition can be held in several dissimilar tasks, like line drawing, walking, getting up and down, with a child at each task.
For: Hyperactive children of all ages.

Equipment: Various materials can be used such as a Ping-Pong ball on a spoon or a bean bag on the head.

Method: Place children on backs, with a bean bag on their heads. See if they can get up keeping bag in place. Have slow races seeing if they can keep bags on head or a small ball on a spoon they are holding.

Modifications: Individual children can be clocked. Slow ascents and descents from mat can be alternated with faster movements. Different tasks can be done at the same time by different children with competition introduced.

For: Hyperactive children of all ages, according to ability.

**Game 4
Don't
Drop
It!**

Equipment: Line, mats.

Method: Pair children off. Have one designated as the slow mover and the other as "his shadow." The shadow tries to match exactly the movements of the other child. Movements must be made slowly to be

**Game 5
Me
and
My
Shadow**

copied. Experiment with a variety of movements.

Modifications: Observer can say whether "shadow" is
really copying correctly; if not, then observer and shadow change roles. Limb
movements, hand-finger movements, and
total body movements can be employed
together or in various combinations.

For: Hyperactive imaginative children of all
ages.

It is not appropriate to teach children simply to move
slowly like zombies as would result if games similar to
Games 3 through 5 only were employed. As can be seen
in Game 6, it may prove helpful, after finding that children can truly control their movements and move slowly,
to vary the speed with which they move—to see whether
they can be excited, aroused, and then bring themselves
"down" again.

**Game 6
Fast
and
Slow**

Equipment: Blackboard, mats, lines.

Method: After children develop a minimum of self-
control, see if they can vary force and
speed and then return to controlled movement ("How slowly can you get up? Now
how fast can you get down?" "Run as fast
as you can from here to there and then
move as slowly as possible").

Modifications: Both fast and slow races can be introduced. The child can be asked to alternate slow and fast tasks that are dissimilar ("Walk the line slowly and then get down fast." "Draw slowly and then run fast"). These activities are effective if carried out to music of various speeds and intensities.

For: Hyperactive children of all ages.

Games of this type are most effective if the child is given concrete evidence of just how slowly he is moving. Stopwatches, graphs, and other indications of increased success, are vital to eliciting improvement. A similar important motivator can be the social approval of the teacher after the child has achieved increased success. Experimenters have also found that candy rewards or checkmarks that can be traded for toys also elicit better control of behavior in activities of this nature.

In addition to the games indicated, it is helpful to ask a child to continue a task for increased periods of time. This is usually most successful if the task is reasonably challenging such as walking a balance beam over obstacles placed on it, instead of simply traversing the beam without any impediments. If the task is too simple or not challenging enough, the child either loses interest and refuses to perform, or while performing is able to attend to objects and events that are extraneous to the task at hand.

Tasks of this nature are helpful in the control of behavior because their execution is easily observed; it is obvious when children stop doing whatever they are doing or when they speed up in Games 3, 4, and 5. It is sometimes difficult to determine whether a child is giving his visual attention to his classroom work.

A legitimate question is whether practicing the games outlined on these pages really reduces unnecessary activity in a classroom, and it is believed that further research is needed to completely confirm their validity in this regard. At the same time, the evidence cited, which may be more thoroughly explored in the references listed at the end of the chapter, seems to offer real hope for those using these techniques. In a recent investigation, for example, it was found that measures of impulse control, including tasks in which children were asked to walk a line as slowly as they could, to draw a line on a blackboard, and to rise in a similar manner, did reflect their teacher's ratings of just how self-controlled they were in a classroom; most helpful as a predictor was the line-drawing task.

However, being able to predict classroom behavior from these tasks does not mean that improved performance of the "how slow can you move?" games will result in appreciable change in the total behavior of the children participating. It is believed, however, that the methods outlined in this chapter do offer a good deal of hope to those who use them correctly and apply them to children whose self-control problems are obvious.

Children Who Are Too Calm

Although the introduction to the chapter mentioned that some children are too "dreamy" or "turned off" to work well in classroom, no space has been devoted to correcting their general behavioral problem.[2]

However, it is far easier to arouse children than to calm them down. Most vigorous activities will accomplish this. Often apparently lethargic children may suffer from hormonal or dietary deficiencies that should be thoroughly explored by the family physician. If medical attention does not correct the problem, the child might then be exposed to the vigorous activities mentioned above. One teacher with whom I am acquainted, for example, places the lethargic child on a small square board with a small raised portion under the middle of the board and asks the child to turn and to twist his body until he becomes more aware to what is happening around him.

---

[2] Many authorities feel that general activation levels are, to some degree, inherited, as marked differences in activity levels are seen in babies at birth—differences that are markedly similar in identical twins, and that persist into early childhood and even into adulthood.

CRATTY, B. J., and SISTER M. M. MARTIN, *Perceptual-Motor Efficiency in Children.* Philadelphia: Lea & Febiger, Publishers, 1969.

———, SISTER M. M. MARTIN, NAMIKO IKEDA, MARGARET MORRIS, and CLAIRE JENNETT, *Movement Activities, Motor Ability and the Education of Children.* Springfield, Ill.: Charles C. Thomas, Publishers, 1970.

JACOBSON, EDMUND, *Progressive Relaxation* (2nd ed.). Chicago: University of Chicago Press, 1938.

———, *Anxiety and Tension Control.* Philadelphia: J. B. Lippincott Co., 1964.

———, (Ed.), *Tension in Medicine.* Springfield, Ill.: Charles C. Thomas, Publishers, 1967.

SCHULTZ, JOHANNES, and WOLFGANG LUTHE, *Autogenic Therapy, Vols. I and II.* New York: Grune & Stratton, Inc., 1969.

Chapter 3

Geometric Figures

Tasks designed to heighten the child's ability to recognize and name basic geometric patterns are found in most perceptual training programs. The research indicates that shortly after birth, infants can visually discriminate between circles, squares, and triangles, generally finding the triangle a more intriguing figure than the first two, as they spend more time looking at it.

Most training programs designed to teach children the differences between circles, squares, triangles, half-circles, diamonds, and the like use visual and tactual dicrimination, as well as questions requiring the children to name the various patterns. The games found on the following pages add another dimension to pattern recognition; they involve some type of total body movement that accompanies the child's practice in the recognition and naming of the various configurations.

Practice in recognition of geometric patterns generally leads to improvement in little else, unless transfer to other tasks is specifically incorporated into the training program. It is probably easier for a retarded child or a pre-school child with normal intelligence to discriminate between and to name half a dozen geometric figures than it is to have them differentiate between and to name twenty-six letters of the alphabet plus several dozen numbers. At the same time, learning the names of various geometric figures can be a waste of time, because after all they cannot be used like letters to form words.

Practice in naming geometric patterns can have several "side effects" that may later serve a child when attempting more complex learning problems. Several basic concepts may be taught through practice in pattern recognition and naming. For example:

(1) On learning the basic geometric patterns, their names, and their characteristics, a child can then be taught that letter forms can be constructed from them. He can be made to realize that two half-circles placed correctly can form a *B,* one half-circle placed a certain way is a *B,* while, by modifying squares and rectangles in various ways, he can make *N*s, *M*s, *W*s, *L*s, *E*s, etc. Also, triangles make *A*s if one of their lines is moved upward slightly.

(2) Children taught to look for the basic characteristics of geometric figures are more likely to identify basic characteristics of letters; they are perhaps less likely to be confused when shown an *A* in various styles of type or in script form. A triangle, for example, has the same characteristics whether on a horizontal plane, or placed on a wall, whether it is large or small. This general concept can serve a child in good stead when attempting to remember letter shapes appearing in various forms in various locations. Games 7, 9, 11, and 12 attempt to aid the child to generalize from figure to figure, accounting for similarities of name by searching for common qualities in each. Most of the games include practice of this type, but specifically Games 1, 3, 6, and 7 aid the child to realize that triangles, squares, and other figures possess certain qualities unique only to them.

(3) Pattern recognition may aid a child to form and to identify figures used in drawing practice. Games in which figures are first drawn include Games 6 and 12.

(4) In the games that follow, a child practices selecting basic geometric figures out of a more complex background. This same problem, selecting a simple word shape out of a configuration of many words on a page, is believed by some to be one of the more important skills needed when initially attempting to read. Game 9 contains an exercise of this type.

The games are meant to be fun. They certainly should not be played for prolonged periods of time. Our research tells us that pattern recognition can be taught using these techniques, and improvement recorded was equal to that seen in children given special small group tutoring in classrooms.

**Game 7
See
and
Match**

Equipment: Patterns on squares, blackboard.

Method: Place two pattern squares at a time in front of the child; draw one of the patterns on blackboard; ask child to jump or hop into correct one, given two choices.

Modifications: Add three squares to choose from, then four, then five. Erase pattern after it is shown to child, and then ask him to jump or hop into proper square containing matching pattern.

For: Normal children 3–6 years, retarded children 6–14 years.

Equipment: Squares with geometric figures on them.

Method: Children jump on each square in order, saying what geometric figure each one is as they land on it. Mix up order of squares after every few children jump on them.

Modifications: If child is correct in two or three, have him draw these on blackboard. Observers check accuracy of children jumping and make corrections when necessary. Have children attempt to change geometric figures on blackboard to standard block letters—making triangle into *A*, half-circles into a *B*, half-circle into a *C*.

For: Normal children 3–6 years, retarded children 5–15 years.

Equipment: Squares containing geometric figures.

Method: Geometric figure is called out while child tries to find it and jump or hop into proper square. Other children check and correct accuracy.

Modifications: Speed up rate of calling. If child is correct, he can draw it on the board and then change geometric figure into letter. Delays of increasing duration can be inserted after figure is called and before response can be made to prolong auditory memory. Children can work in pairs, one calling and the other jumping.

For: Normal children 3–7 years, retarded children 6–15 years.

Game 10
See
and
Throw

Equipment: Squares containing geometric figures, small bean bags (bags can be on strings for handicapped children), blackboard.

Method: Geometric figure is drawn on board and then child tries to find it among several and to throw bean bag into correct one. Other observing children check accuracy.

Modifications: Child can throw first and then say which geometric figure bag landed in. Handicapped child, in wheelchair, can retrieve bag via string and repeat without help from teacher. Child can be given geometric figure auditorily and then try to throw into proper one without any visual comparison on board. Child can be given capital letter on board and then asked to throw it into geometric figure that makes up the letter (D = half-circle, Q = circle, N = square).

For: Normal children 3–7 years, retarded children 6–16 years, physically handicapped children of all ages with ability to use upper limbs.

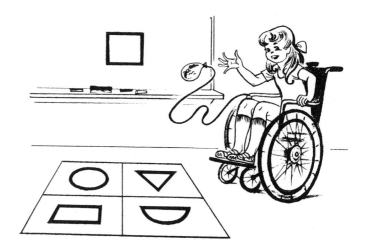

Game 11
Go
and
Get
It

Equipment: Blackboard, squares containing geometric figures.

Method: Children line up with squares placed between them. One figure is called, as, "square." Two children who are then touched by teacher at same time race to see who can retrieve square first and bring it back to line. Winner can draw it on blackboard.

Modifications: Figure is written on board rather than called out. Letter is called out and child must retrieve the geometric figure that will form it with modifications. Children on two teams may be numbered one to five; then teacher may call "two-rectangle," meaning that the number-two child on each team must see who can get the rectangle square first.

For: Normal children 3–7 years, retarded children 6–15 years, handicapped children of all ages with modifications.

Game 12 Cut and Find

Equipment: Scissors, cardboard, blackboard, and squares containing geometric figures.

Method: Children first see figure on blackboard and then cut it out of cardboard and find it on the proper square. One should note similar characteristics of cardboard figure and the one found on the square (number of sides, corners, and so on).

Modifications: On finding the proper square, the child can see how many things he can do to it (hop on it, run around it, jump over it). He also can count sides or corners of both figures to check accuracy. The handicapped child can throw a bean bag into the proper square.

For: Normal youngsters 3–7 years, retarded children 6–16 years, handicapped children of all ages, but specifically those with normal intelligence 4–7 years.

Game 13 Big Things and Little Things

Equipment: Lining tape, cardboard, scissors, blackboard, squares containing geometric figures.

Method: Illustrate that the same figure can be made larger or smaller. Start with jumping into squares containing figures; jump and say what they are; then ask children to either "make larger ones" (with lining tape on playground or gymnasium floor) or smaller ones (drawing on blackboard or cutting them out of cardboard). After this is done, even smaller ones may be cut out or drawn or larger ones made on floor, and games can be played in these larger ones (for example, three-base game on triangle).

Modifications: Larger and smaller may be played just on floor, or on blackboard, drawing same figures of increasing or decreasing size. Discussion should take place concerning characteristics of each geometric figure. Big and little letters may be drawn on blackboard.

For: Normal children 4–8 years, retarded children 6–16 years.

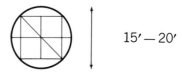

Game 14 Jump and Tape

Equipment: Squares containing geometric figures, yellow lining tape two inches wide, blackboard.

Facilities: Playground with yellow-lined, large geometric figures of all types.

Method: Child draws figure asked for on a blackboard, runs to proper square containing same figure, jumps into it, and then finds even larger figure on playground. If it is not there, he may then use lining tape and make his own figure on a playground or on the gymnasium floor.

Modifications: Child may be asked to invent games on one of the larger geometric figures. He may be asked to do three or more things within one of the figures (to walk their edges and count sides or figures on playground, to modify figures into letters using additional pieces of lining tape, for example, changing rectangle into *M, N, L,* or *H*).

For: Normal children 4–8 years, retarded children 6–16 years.

Equipment: Complex figure, containing all standard geometric figures as shown. Squares containing geometric figures, blackboard.

**Game 15
Find
It
In
the
Maze**

Method: Child is shown a single figure or it is called out, and then he must run through the corresponding figure within the complex figure maze.

Modifications: Child must first jump into square containing figure, say what it is, and then run through it on larger complex pattern. Child may run through all figures on complex pattern, calling them out as he moves. Child first runs through figure and then draws it on board, and then perhaps changes it into letter shape on board. Child in wheelchair may ask partner to push him through proper pathways while giving directions to him.

For: Normal children 3–7 years, retarded children 6–15 years.

**Game 16
Find
It
and
Do
It,
In
Order**

Equipment: Squares containing geometric figures.

Method: Arrange squares in half-circle; ask children to jump or to do something in each and then ask other children to copy them; use two, three, four, and then five squares in this manner. Child may do "his own thing" in each square and then either repeat these himself or request another child in the class to copy him exactly; first child acts as evaluator. Each time a square is jumped on, it must be named (circle, half-circle, and so on).

Modifications: Use a ball and do something to each square with a ball (roll it over, bounce it, dribble it around). Call out geometric figure when each is approached.

For: Normal children 3–8 years, retarded children 5–16 years, handicapped children using bean bags on strings, all ages.

**Game 17
Left
Things
and
Right
Things**

Equipment: Square containing geometric figures, blackboard.

Method: Children jump, hop using one foot, or do something to each square when encountered. They both identify square's geometric figure and also say whether they are doing a "right" thing or a "left" thing (hopping into it with a right foot, jumping around it to the left side).

Modifications: Handicapped child in wheelchair may be asked whether his bean bag landed to the left or right of the center of each square aimed at, as well as being asked the name of the geometric figure in each square. Children may observe and evaluate each other's efforts ("Is it really to the left (or right)?" "Is it truly a circle?" "Is it truly a half-circle with which you are dealing?").

For: Normal children 3–8 years, retarded children 9–16 years, handicapped children all ages.

**Game 18
Lots
of
Things**

Equipment: Squares containing geometric figures, cardboard, scissors, bean bag with string attached.

Method: Children cut out all geometric figures into sizes about three inches by three inches. While holding the *M* in their hand, they attempt to jump to correct matching square holding same figure in the correct order (as each one is landed in, child shuffles another one to the top in his hand-held packet, finds its match by jumping in it, and then places another small square on the top, finds it, and continues).

Modifications: Child in wheelchair can shuffle them in his - lap and then try to throw bean bag into correct square. After retrieving it, a second and a third pattern can be thrown.

For: Normal children 3–7 years, retarded children 7–16 years, physically handicapped children all ages.

Summary

These games are intended to aid children to perceptually and cognitively identify various geometric figures. Some of the activities in turn help the child to transfer his ability to name a triangle into more helpful skills involving letter recognition and number recognition. Additionally, the games aid a child to integrate information obtained tactually and visually with impressions gained as the children move their bodies through space.

Bibliography

UHR, LEONARD, (Ed.), *Pattern Recognition.* New York: John Wiley & Sons, Inc., 1966.

Chapter 4

Remembering Things

Remembering a series of items is an everyday necessity. Phone numbers must be memorized, spelling and counting must be mastered, and directions must be remembered.

A great deal is known about people's ability to remember verbal information. Lists of nonsense syllables have been the subject of innumerable learning studies published in psychological journals since before the turn of the 20th century. Within recent years, the ability of children to learn and to retain information of various kinds has been accorded increasing attention. My colleagues and I have found that practice in remembering correctly a series of movements performed by another child and in repeating these movements contributed positively to the children's ability to remember a series of pictures, words, and letters. In this same study we found high to moderate correlations among scores in serial memory tasks regardless of what was to be remembered.

Our observations have further suggested that it is easier for a child to perform a series of movements and then to remember and to again perform these same movements in the same order than it is for a child to observe another and then to copy his same movements in the same order. We have also noted that the type of game outlined in this chapter is highly motivating to children. They request this kind of task again and again, and we have often used it as a reward for good work at the end of the learning sessions.

It will usually be found that movements toward the middle of a series will be harder for a child to duplicate than the first and final movements in the series. A similar phenomenon has been noted when researching the retention of pieces of verbal information.

As can be seen when scanning the following games, several purposes can be served. For example, several games (Games 19, 24, and so on) employ numbers, letters, and geometric figures. Other games test a child in his ability to remember a series of locations (Games 19, 27, and 28) rather than a series of movements made in a given order.

It is also apparent on examining the games that activities of this nature can be made extremely difficult. By requiring a child to perform, to remember a number of things in each configuration, and/or to remember both movements and locations in order, his intellect will be severely taxed.[1]

Several of the games (Games 19, 21, and 22) involve remembering verbal descriptions of movements rather than simply the visual representations of the actions performed. Many speech teachers throughout the country utilize games of this nature to improve the language skills of normal and atypical children.

Problems in left-right discrimination can also be worked on within the games as shown; an example is Game 25. Ball-handling skills can also be improved using these kinds of serial memory tasks, as can be seen in Game 23.

Although the illustrations generally show the use of two-dimensional obstacles (lines and configurations on a flat surface), these same games can be played using three-

[1]Tasks involving serial memory are usually found in IQ tests.

dimensional obstacles (tires, boxes, bars, tree trunks, and the like). It should also be noted that the obstacles, whether two- or three-dimensional, are usually arranged in a semicircular pattern. In this manner it is possible, we believe, to maintain better class control than would be the case if children, when finishing their "trip," ended up a linear distance away from their starting point. Arranged in this way, the games also permit a better view to the observing children.

Serial memory ability is closely related to perceptual span. The latter quality involves the ability to quickly and accurately count and/or otherwise identify a group of configurations when only given a brief instant to inspect them. It is believed that innumerable qualities can be enhanced using these interesting games; many more modifications are possible than are contained in the following pages.

In a recent investigation conducted in selected Catholic elementary schools in Los Angeles, practice in the type of serial memory tasks described in this chapter was found to have several outcomes: (a) The children's ability to remember a series of movements changed from an average of slightly over three to almost six by the end of the semester. (b) Their ability to remember and to repeat a series of numbers, given verbally, in correct order showed similar improvement. (c) Their ability to remember and to place in correct order a series of pictures presented visually also improved significantly, as contrasted with the performance of control groups who had no practice in "movement" serial memory tasks. Most important is the fact that the two serial memory tasks described in (b) and (c) above were not engaged in during the semester-long training period.

**Game 19
Where
Did
I
Visit?**

Equipment: Lining tape, squares containing geometric figures placed as shown.

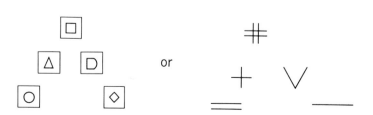

Method: Child "visits" each square or configuration, not necessarily in order (he might visit three or four), and then he tries to repeat the visits in the same order (running and standing in each configuration or square).

Modifications: Another child observing the first child's order of visits tries to repeat visits in the same order. A third child may act as evaluator, judging the accuracy of the efforts of the first child to repeat his own visits in correct order, or the efforts of the second child in repeating correctly the visits of the first child. More and more configurations may be added.

For: Normal children 3–8 years, retarded children 6–16 years, handicapped children (throwing bean bags into configurations in a given order) all ages.

**Game 20
Repeat
Myself**

Equipment: Lining tape as shown, lines about two feet long, figures about two feet apart.

Method: Child does three or four things to each configuration and then tries to repeat exactly the same things himself. Observing teacher or another child evaluates the accuracy of his efforts. He may hop, jump, run around, jump into, and so forth.

Modifications: May do movements backward (jump backward, sideways, with one foot, turning movements). Figures may be added to form six or seven configurations.

For: Normal children 2–7 years, retarded children 6–9 years.

Equipment: Squares containing geometric patterns or tape making configurations similar to those shown in Games 19 and 20.

Method: Child visits (hops or jumps there) each of three or four configurations not necessarily in order. Second observing child either instructs the first child where he went as he tries to repeat himself or verbally informs a third child where the first child "visited" and in what order.

Modifications: Number of configurations visited can be increased; what was done in each may be made different; (hop in one, jump in a second, and so on). Order can be changed after each turn.

For: Children with normal intelligence 3–8 years, retarded children 5–16 years, hand-

Game 21
Tell
Me
Where
I
Went

icapped children (throwing bean bags into configurations in various orders) all ages.

**Game 22
Tell
Me
What
I
Did**

Equipment: Squares containing geometric figures or tape forming configurations similar to previous games (Games 19 and 20).

Method: First child does something to one, two, or three configurations (hops in one, jumps around second, jumps into third). Observing child tells the first child what he did and instructs him verbally as he tries to repeat the same movements in the same order on the same configurations.

Modifications: A third child may, with instructions from the observer, try to duplicate what the first child did in correct order.

For: Normal children 3–8 years, retarded children 6–16 years.

**Game 23
Ball
Things**

Equipment: Lining tape or squares containing geometric patterns arranged in semicircle as shown in Games 19 and 20, using three to seven patterns or squares. Two or three eight-inch-diameter rubber playground balls.

Method: A child does something with a ball in each configuration (or square) in order (bounces it in 1, rolls it over 2, and so on). Second observing child tries to repeat what was done, in the same order, at each configuration. First child observes him and instructs him when errors are observed.

Modifications: A third child can continue to act as an observer and either correct the evaluator or instruct other children in exactly what the first child did. This instruction can be verbal (to aid in language development), can be demonstrated, or can be both demonstrated and described.

For: Normal children 3–9 years, retarded children 6–16 years.

Equipment: Serial memory configurations as shown in Games 19 and 20, composed either of squares containing letters, numbers, geometric figures, or configurations made of tape as shown.

Game 24
Add
One

5			Q	T	

| 3 | 4 | or | 2 | | B | or |

| 1 | | 2 | A | | C | X |

$$+$$ $$\vee$$

$$=$$ $$\triangle$$

Method: First child does something to one configuration; second child repeats what first child did and adds another to the second figure; third child copies first two movements on first two configurations and then adds his own movement to the third.

Modifications: May use ball; do a left or right thing; simply visit one, two, or three or more stations in an irregular order (not necessarily starting with first one to the right, with the second and subsequent children trying to remember where previous ones visited and then adding a visit of their own).

For: Normal children 4–10 years, retarded children 6–16 years, handicapped children (with visits made by bean bag thrown and then retrieved using attached string) all ages.

**Game 25
Left
and
Right**

Equipment: Serial memory squares or taped configurations as shown in Game 6.

Method: First child does a left thing or right thing in each of four to six configurations (jumps with left foot, runs around second to the right) and is asked to tell whether he is going to the left or the right. Observing teacher or another child (should have a mental age above nine years) tells whether responses are correct.

Modifications: Observing child may attempt to repeat in correct order the responses of the first performing child. Observing child may try to tell a third child what the first child did, as the third child attempts to duplicate first's responses correctly. A follow-the-leader game might be started, with each child attempting to do what the child ahead of him does.

For: Normal children and retarded children with mental ages at or above 6 years.

Equipment: Tape, squares containing letters, numbers, or geometric configurations.

Method: Children are allowed to place tape or squares in the order they decide upon. They then jump into them, calling out their characteristics if they are letter, number, or geometric-figure squares. They then mix them up and see if observing children can place them in the same order and jump into them the same way.

Modifications: Interpolate taped figures between squares that are movable; keep taped figures intact. Do more than one thing to each square; visit squares in different orders (not in the order they are placed next to each other).

For: Normal children 4–10 years, retarded children 6–16 years.

**Game 26
Arrange
and
Show**

Equipment: Letter, number, or geometric squares arranged as shown in Game 24 or taped configurations; balls, ropes, and so on.

Method: Child does more than one thing at each configuration and visits from two to four configurations. Observing child attempts to duplicate order of visits, plus what was done at each configuration or square. He might do a ball thing and a jumping thing at each configuration or square or perhaps three things at each stop.

Modifications: Child might try to duplicate his own things. Observing child might try to verbalize and tell a third child what the first child did at each stop.

For: Normal children 5–10 years, retarded children 7–15 years. Handicapped children (using more than one bean bag attached to strings with bags of various colors, throwing bags in various orders at each configuration) all ages. (Note: An observing handicapped child might attempt to duplicate throwing order and targets in order.)

**Game 27
Many
Things**

Game 28
Many
Things
At
Many
Places

Equipment: Letter, number, or geometric squares and/ or configurations of tape as shown in Game 24.

Method: At each configuration place a performing child and an observing child, whose job it is to watch the performer do three to six things and then to repeat these same things in order.

Modifications: Gradually raise the number of things done; change configurations by moving observer-performing team or by moving one of the team, keeping the other member fixed. Reverse roles of observer and performer.

For: Normal children 5–12 years, retarded children 6–16 years.

Summary

Serial memory games have been found to be highly motivating and helpful to children. The combinations of games may be used to enhance memory, left-right discrimination, geometric-figure, letter, and number identification. Observational skills as well as language skills may be incorporated by the imaginative teacher into some of the activities described. Increasing difficulty can be introduced by having a child try to remember an increasing number of things or by requiring a child to remember and duplicate complex movements of another child.

Research data have indicated that practice in remembering a series of movements executed by another child can transfer positively to serial memory tasks in which numbers are given verbally, and must be repeated verbally; and tasks in which visually presented pictures must be remembered and placed in correct order.

Chapter 5

Numbers and Counting

The games in this chapter are intended to help children place verbal labels on various numbers and to demonstrate that numbers can be in various places and still be called the same number (on blackboards, within complex line shapes, and on the jumping squares). More important, however, many of the games are designed to help children grasp quantitative concepts. Game 35, "Spaceship," illustrates to the child quite clearly that 3 is indeed different quantitatively from 1, as it is three times farther from the beginning of the ship to the third square than it is to the first square. Various other games, notably Games 32, 41, and 43, also incorporate counting into activities that involve quantitative concepts (for example, how far can you jump?).

Most of the games provide an opportunity for the child to write and to visually observe the letter in forms other than those on the squares or playground configurations on which they may jump. Hopefully the children will be able to generalize concerning the basic qualitative differences between numbers—as well as the basic qualities possessed by each number—no matter where a number appears, how large it is, or how it is written.

Many of the games involve numbers having more than one digit. Game 33 is an example of this type. In some cases, the tasks permit a child to move to a given number; in other cases numbers can be carried in various relay situations.

Younger children frequently write their numbers backward. This in fact is the rule rather than the exception in the case of children of five. Six-year-old children will also evidence this tendency at times, but children by the age of seven are less likely to do so. This type of error may be corrected by playing a lot of left-right games, some of which are outlined in the serial memory chapter, and then teaching the child in just what direction each number that is asymmetrical(that is, 2, 3, 4, 5, 6, 7, and 9) must face. Modifications of some of the games may also correct this tendency. For example, a child may, as he lands in a number square, not only call out the number but say in which direction some part of the number faces (i.e., "the straight, long part of the number 4 is to the right," or "the open part of the 3 is to the left").

Some of the games, such as Game 34, are extremely difficult. Running through a letter shape without any visual guides is almost impossible for children under the age of eight.

The final games in this series lead logically toward the mathematical operations in Chapter 6.

**Game 29
Look
and
Match**

Equipment: Number squares, blackboard.

Method: Two squares are placed on the ground in front of a child or two children. A number is written on the board, and the child (or children) must jump into the appropriate matching number in front of him.

Modifications: Increase the number of numbers from which to choose; write a number and then erase it for increasing periods of time be-

fore permitting movement response to correct larger square (i.e., jumping).

For: Normal children 3–7 years, retarded children 5–15 years, and handicapped children of all ages, depending on mental ability.

Equipment: Number squares, blackboard.

**Game 30
Hear,
Say,
and
Jump**

1	5	4	3	5	7	0
6	0	2	7	8	9	8
9	5	6	4	3	1	3
4	2	4	2	6	3	2
1	8	5	7	0	9	1

Method: Teacher or student teacher says a number, and child must find it on the grid containing numbers and jump into the appropriate matching number.

Modifications: More than one number can be called at a time, and child must find two, three, four or more numbers in this manner. An increasing number of choices can be placed in front of the child. A time lapse can be introduced between hearing the number(s) and the movement response produced by the child or children.

For: Normal children 3–8 years, retarded children 5–15 years, handicapped children (throwing bean bags into appropriate squares) of all ages depending on mental ability.

**Game 31
Drawing,
Touching,
and
Jumping**

Equipment: Cardboard, scissors, squares containing numbers.

Method: Numbers can be cut out, written on board, talked about, touched, and then found and jumped in on the grid.

Modifications: Retarded children can spend a day or a week on a single number in this manner. Children can hold up a cut-out number and then ask a partner to find it on the square and jump into it. Numbers can be written in various sizes, can be cut out in various sizes, and then jumped into or hopped into in various ways on the grids.

For: Normal children 3–8 years, retarded children 5–15 years, handicapped children of all ages.

**Game 32
Run
Through
It**

Equipment: Lined configurations, using lining tape, painted lines, or grooves made in a large sandbox; blackboard.

Method: Number is either called verbally or written on board. Child must then find it by running through its configuration within the more complex patterns. Increasing difficulty can be elicited if the child must run his own pattern without any guides (i.e., on an unmarked grass or cement area or when more than one number at a time is called and then more than one is "traced" via running movements). Children can also jump, hop, skip, move backward, or otherwise negotiate the appropriate pattern.

Modifications: Child can first write number on a card and then, holding it, try to run through appropriate pattern. Number can be erased prior to jumping in it or hopping in it.

For: Normal children 3–8 years, retarded children 5–15 years, handicapped children of all ages.

Game 33
More
Numbers,
Many
Digits

Equipment: Blackboard, number squares.

Method: Two-digit or three-digit numbers are written on blackboard. Child must jump into both digits or place one foot in one and the second in the other. If three or four or more digit numbers are used, child may either jump into each in order or place a hand, foot, and foot in the three if possible.

Modifications: Numbers may be given verbally and then found in the above manner. One child may find two or three numbers in order on the jumping grids and then, observing another child or children, must say which numbers they are (i.e., 10, 131, etc.).

For: Normal children 3–8 years, retarded children 7–17 years, handicapped children of all ages when capable.

Game 34
Running
In
the
Sand

Equipment: Blackboard, sandbox.

Method: Child must run through a number's shape in the sandbox after first hearing it or seeing it written on the blackboard.

Modifications: Races of this nature can take place using two or more children at the same time or at different times. Numbers can be first run through and then written on the board; written numbers can be erased for increasing periods of time before permitting children to run through them in the sand. The child can hold a series of cards in his hand, containing all numbers, and at the same time try to run through each one in order, shuffling to the top of the pile the card containing the number dealt with.

For: Normal children 4–8 years, retarded children 8–18 years, handicapped children with modifications (i.e., they can be observers or "student teachers" for the more physically capable).

Game 35
Spaceship

Equipment: Blackboard, a spaceship as shown done with a painted line or with lining tape.

| 10 | 9 | 8 | 7 | 6 | 5 | 4 | 3 | 2 | 1 |

Method: Practice jumping along the numbers and counting while executing the countdown and blasting off the spaceship. Observing children can check accuracy.

Modifications: Handicapped children can throw balls or bean bags in order in each square, calling out appropriate number as they land in each one. Numbers can be done in any order. Number can be written on board and then found on the spaceship or vice versa. When a number is jumped in and named correctly, the child can then write it on the board.

For: Normal children 3–8 years, retarded children 6–16 years, handicapped children of all ages (with the modifications outlined above).

**Game 36
Counting
Relays**

Equipment: Two or more sets of number squares, blackboard.

Method: One member at a time from each of two teams runs to a location, finds a number (starting with 1), returns to his team with the number, places it on the ground, and tags the next team member, who returns to same location and obtains the second number in order (i.e., 2), who repeats process. Winning team finishes first. More than nine members on a team may be used if numbering is either started over again after reaching 9 or if two squares are obtained.

Modifications: Children may be asked to jump, hop, or skip for letters. Two children at a time from each team may go for a single letter, each holding it when returning on the run. The number may be obtained in random order, triggered by series of numbers on the blackboard (i.e., 6859321).

For: Normal children 3–8 years, retarded children 7–15 years, handicapped children who may obtain letters in wheelchairs by being pushed by more capable children.

Equipment: Two or more grids containing all numbers of individual squares.

Method: One member at a time from each of two teams runs to grid and jumps into appropriate squares (i.e., first 1, then 2, etc.). Then he returns to his team, tags the next child, etc., until all numbers are used. Two-digit numbers may also be used (tenth child must jump into 1 and 0 squares, eleventh into 1 and 1 squares, etc.). Counting backward can also be used (100–1).

Modifications: Numbers, either one- or two-digit, may be executed by the teams in random order with the numbers placed on a blackboard in front of the teams. Numbers can be alternated (i.e., 1 on board, 2 jumped into, 3 written, 4 jumped into, etc.).

For: Normal children 3–8 years, retarded children 7–15 years, handicapped children (throwing bean bags into appropriate squares) of all ages.

**Game 37
Run
and
Jump,
Counting
Relays**

Equipment: Grid containing number squares.

Method: One or more children, using one or several grids, jump from 1 to any other number in order. They may count to any number in this manner, using two- and then three-digit numbers. Count out loud as number is landed in; observing children check accuracy.

Modifications: Speed races may be held against each other or against a clock (i.e., "How fast can you count to 50 by jumping in the appropriate squares in the right order?").

For: Normal children 4–8 years, retarded children 6–16 years, handicapped children (with modifications) of all ages.

**Game 38
Jump
and
Count**

Equipment: Flash cards containing numbers, number squares.

Method: Number is flashed briefly, and child must make response into appropriate matching square on the grid (i.e., hop into it).

**Game 39
See
Quick
and
Hop**   55

Modifications: A time lapse may be introduced after the flash card is seen. The flash can be accompanied by verbal identification of the number by child and/or by teacher.

For: Normal children 5–8 years, retarded children 6–16 years, handicapped children of all ages.

**Game 40
Partner
Write
and
Tell**

Equipment: Blackboard(s), grids containing large number squares.

Method: Children work in partners. One jumps and the other writes a number on the board. Child may first jump and then write, or the writing child can cue the jumping child as to what to do. Competing teams can see who can finish a series of numbers first (i.e., numbers written on card for team member using blackboard).

Modifications: Writing partner can both write and say number, or he can be required to write number and then erase it prior to asking partner to jump into square. He can write one number and make the game adding a given number to it each time (i.e., write 2, but must add 3 before jumping response, 5).

For: Normal children 4—8 years, retarded children 6—16 years, handicapped children of all ages (wheelchair child can write or may find larger number by throwing bean bag, etc.).

Equipment: Number squares.

Method: Each child has his own number square and must execute three, four, or five things into or around each square. He chooses his own things (i.e., jump into it, jump on it forward, hop over it, run around it). There are thousands of possibilities. An observing child counts the responses of the moving child, and then the roles are reversed.

**Game 41
How
Many
Can
You?**

Modifications: The size of the number may signal the number of things required (i.e., the 3 square means you must do three things to it). Children may move from smaller to larger numbers in this manner. Children should be given time to think of their own things in this game.

For: Normal children 5–12 years, retarded children 6–16 years, handicapped children of all ages as capable.

Game 42 How Many Did I?

Equipment: Number squares.

Method: Similar to Game 41, but children compete in teams of two or more to see how many different things they can do to their numbers. The team or individual thinking of the most original things is the winner. Observing children judge originality.

Modifications: You might limit what they may do to specific categories (i.e., one-legged things, blackboard things, jumping things, going around things).

For: Children with normal mentality, 3–13 years, retarded children 5–16 years, handicapped children as capable.

Game 43 How Far Can You Jump?

Equipment: Twenty lines, about three inches long, placed two inches apart. They are made with tape or paint on a mat, floor, or cement surface.

Method: After a standing broadjump is executed, children determine how far they went by counting lines they traversed. Competition can be introduced; backward broadjumping can be a modification; sideways jumping for distance can also be used. Actual distance can be computed by multiplying lines by 2.

Modifications: Child can experiment with various arm movements while jumping (i.e., leaving them down at sides, throwing them upward or forward and upward). Self-esti-

mation of future success can take place prior to first jump and before successive attempts. Measurement between estimations and actual performance may be most revealing. Ball thrown for distance can be done in a similar manner, using a long tape measure.

For: Normal children 5–15 years, retarded children 7–17 years, handicapped children as capable (or may serve as scorers).

Summary

The tasks outlined in this chapter have been intended to inculcate two types of abilities: (1) the operation in which children translate a number shape into the names of numbers, and (2) the concept that a number stands for a given quantity and the comparison of number quantities.

Chapter 6

Mathematics

Virtually any mathematical operation can be employed in some kind of movement task. However, to do so may at times be inefficient, clumsy, and really unnecessary. Yet, the variety of games illustrated in this chapter can be expanded almost indefinitely, particularly by a creative teacher.

The final three games in this series can involve observation of an athletic contest, rather than direct participation. The number squares, including squares containing the standard arithmetical signs (−, +, =, ×, ÷) and some squares containing pictures of objects (i.e., rabbits) make it possible to "jump out" in a rather concrete way various mathematics problems.

Some of the games permit either the answer or the problem to be presented via total body movement. It has been found that the most involvement occurs when the children act as teachers. Children seem to like these games so much that they will prefer difficult tasks over easy and thus uninteresting operations.

It has been possible in many of these games to construct situations in which reasonably concrete problems can be carried out. For example, Games 45, 46, and 52 are conducted in this manner.

Several of the games involve some kind of self-testing on the part of the children and thus can evaluate fitness as well as provide the impetus for various standard physical education improvement programs. Game 49, involving a jump-reach test, and Game 52, involving broadjumping, are of this type.

Omitted in the games is a direct reference to some of the concepts found in the "new math." However, the creative teacher using this program can easily modify some of the existing games to meet her needs. Algebra problems are also not found extensively in the following games but can be easily played with the addition of various letter squares (i.e., $5 = a + 3$). Game 56 is an example of this type, and others could be adapted in this manner.

Several of the games resemble traditional playground games for elementary school children. The movement in the game is governed by the children's ability to "come up" with correct answers to mathematics problems expressed verbally or in written form. Game 54 is of this type.

Equipment: Number squares containing numbers and arithmetical signs ($=$, $+$, $-$, $\div$, $\times$).

Method: Using the squares, children are verbally told the name of a sign and must find it by jumping into it on the grid. Discussion should continue to define the operation or operations indicated by the sign.

Modifications: Advanced children can continue on and jump simple addition and subtraction problems (i.e., $2 + 2 = 4$) by hopping in the appropriate squares. Or, they can act out operations by using blank squares and

Game 44
Find
the
Sign

carrying them apart and together when adding or subtracting operations are discussed.

For: Normal children 6–12 years, retarded children 7–15 years, handicapped children as capable.

**Game 45
Collect
and
Count**

Equipment: Letter squares or blank squares.

Method: Children run to a central pile of squares, gather two or more, return and collect more, and count each group they collect. Each time they return with their squares, they count the number they have added together.

Modifications: Other children, by jumping in appropriate squares, may cue the running children as to how many squares to bring back. They then can jump the answer to the simple addition problem as the other children are counting the squares to obtain the answer.

For: Normal children 7–12 years, retarded children 8–15 years, handicapped children as capable.

Equipment: Squares, either blank or containing numbers and letters.

Method: Children start with a pile of five or six squares and then take away one or more squares, counting first the initial number and then the final number.

Modifications: Children can cue one another concerning the original number, how many to take away, and the expected answer, by jumping into the appropriate numbers on a letter grid containing larger squares.

For: Normal children 7 and older, retarded children 8 and older, handicapped children as capable.

**Game 46
Take
Away
the
Squares**

Equipment: Blackboard and squares containing numbers and signs.

Method: A simple problem in addition or subtraction is placed on the board, and children try to jump into number squares indicating the correct answer. Two-digit answers

**Game 47
Jump
the
Answer**

63

can be indicated by separate movements or by placing each foot in a separate square.

Modifications: Children can give problems verbally to one another or can write them on the board. Problems of increased complexity can be offered in this manner. Competition for speed of correct answers can be introduced between two or more children. Observing children can verify correctness of answers of jumping or hopping children.

For: Normal children 7–12 years, retarded children 8–16 years, handicapped children (with modifications) as capable.

**Game 48
Hop
the
Problems**

Equipment: Blackboard, grid containing number squares.

Method: Child jumps a problem using number grids containing appropriate signs (plus and minus). Observing child, at another grid or at a blackboard, indicates the answer (i.e., by writing or by jumping into

appropriate squares). Thus a problem is jumped out in concrete terms $(2 + 2 = \underline{\quad})$.

Modifications: Children can attempt to first write and then duplicate a problem by jumping in squares. Subtraction and addition can be made even more concrete by having squares containing pictures of rabbits, etc., so that the child can be jumping 2 rabbits + 4 rabbits = 6 rabbits. Observing children can check correctness of problems and responses.

For: Normal children 7 and older, retarded children 8 and older, handicapped children as capable.

Equipment: Twenty lines placed one or two inches apart on the vertical surface of a gymnasium wall or on a classroom wall.

Method: Start at about head level with the shortest child in the class. The child first stands against the wall, with both toes against it,

**Game 49
Jump
and
Reach**

and reaches upward, arms straight, to see how high he can reach. He then turns to the side and tries to jump and touch as far above his standing-plus-reach height as he can. Score is computed by subtracting standing reach from jumping reach.

For: Normal children 6–16 years, retarded children 8–16 years, handicapped children as capable (or as scorers).

**Game 50
Addition
Relays**

Equipment: Grids containing squares with numbers and mathematical signs.

Method: One member at a time from each of two teams jumps out a problem in his grid. The second member from each team jumps out the answer. A checker from the opposite team determines the accuracy of the response. This procedure continues, problem alternated with answer, until all members of the team are finished and the winning team is determined by

speed and accuracy. Inaccurate answers must be rejumped by the child after being corrected.

Modifications: Team members may have to run, hop, or in some other way move a distance to the grid prior to executing the problem and answer.

For: Normal children 8 and older, retarded children 10 and older, handicapped children as capable.

Equipment: Blackboard, grids containing numbers (one for each team).

Method: Both teams start with 100 points. A member from each team runs to his grid and jumps into a one-digit number, which is subtracted by another team member on the blackboard from 100. The next team members run and jump into a second number, which is subtracted from this

Game 51
Subtraction
Runs

first remainder. This procedure continues until all team members compete one or more times. Accuracy is checked on by observers. The last child running becomes the subtractor at the blackboard and then returns to the end of the line.

Modifications: Teams may work in pairs, one observing and the other jumping. Teams may start with 1,000 or more points and jump two-digit numbers before subtracting them each time.

For: Normal children 8 and older, retarded children 10 and older, handicapped children as capable.

**Game 52
Take
Away
Broadjumps**

Equipment: Twenty three-inch lines placed one or two inches apart on a horizontal surface (the floor of a gymnasium, a classroom, a cement surface, or a mat).

Method: Children, one at a time, execute a standing broadjump to see how far they can travel.

They use the lines to land on and measure their jumps. Next, starting from the same point, they execute a backward broad-jump. Subtract the two scores to find the difference.

Modifications: To find out the effects of learning, they may also subtract their first attempt at either forward or backward broadjumping from the final attempt.

For: Normal children 7 and older, retarded children 9 and older, handicapped children as capable (or can act as recorders).

Equipment: Tape measure 100–150 feet long, balls of various kinds and sizes.

Method: Children should be permitted to throw along the length of the tape to see how far they can throw using various techniques (i.e., underhand, using a run into the throw, overhand, using a step into the throw) and various different sizes of balls.

**Game 53
Throwing
Best
Subtraction**

Subtraction problems of a wide variety can then be computed on a blackboard to compare the distances thrown with various kinds of balls.

Modifications: Throwing contests can be run. Children can look at learning improvement using various techniques, comparing first attempts to subsequent efforts.

For: Normal children 7–18 years, retarded children 9 and older, and handicapped children as capable (or may act as scorers and recorders).

**Game 54
Decimal
Races**

Equipment: Stopwatches, running surface 30–100 yards long, score cards, clipboards.

Method: Take team scores in running a given distance, by addition of tenths of seconds, of all members' efforts (i.e., low score wins).

Modifications: Course can be circular. Distances can vary for various group members with different capabilities. Each member can get three or more trials and his best trial computed for the team effort. Children can hop, skip, or otherwise negotiate the course.

For: Normal children 8 and older, retarded children 10 and older, handicapped children as capable (or as scorers).

**Game 55
Team
Base
Count
and
Add**

Equipment: Diamond with three or four bases, playground ball, blackboard or numbers in grid.

Method: The team up hits, one at a time sending the ball to the outfield. The team in the field retrieves the ball, lines up behind one another, with the retriever in the front of line, and passes the ball quickly to the rearmost member, who yells "Stop." The hitter circles as many bases as possible, continuing past home if he is able and making additional circuits of the bases. A progressive score is kept on the black-board of all team members' efforts. Then the fielding team goes to bat.

Modifications: Score can also be kept on grid, or child on grid can jump into squares corresponding to bases passed by runner. Children can hop, skip, or do something other than run bases.

For: Normal children 6 and older, retarded children 8 and older, handicapped children.

Equipment: Blackboard, grids containing number squares and addition, subtraction, and multiplication signs ($+$, $-$, $\times$).

Method: A multiplication problem is placed on the blackboard. Children singly or in competition with one another try to jump the proper answer. Use one-digit numbers to work on multiplication problem. May be

**Game 56
Time-Tables
Leap**

alternated with addition or subtraction problems.

Modifications: Problems can be given via another child jumping into squares in grid. Answer can appear on board or via jumping or hopping again.

For: Normal children 8 and older, retarded children in their teens, handicapped children as capable.

**Game 57
Hear
and
Hop**

Equipment: Blackboard, grids containing numbers.

Method: Problems (multiplication, simple addition, or subtraction) are given verbally and then answered via jumping in grid or writing on board.

Modifications: Team competitions can be introduced. A problem can be voiced and time intervals introduced. A child, on getting the right answer, can be permitted to give next problem.

For: Normal children 8 and older, retarded children (educables) in their teens, handicapped children as capable.

Equipment: Blackboard, patterns made by painted lines or by lining tape as shown.

**Game 58
Answer
Running**

8 4

Method: A variety of mathematics problems can be given verbally or written on the blackboard. Children, in pairs or alone, can attempt to run through configurations giving answers. Observing children can confirm accuracy. The running child can also voice the answer.

Modifications: A sandbox can be used and the answer run through in sand without any guiding configurations. Relays can be played in this manner, using separate grids for each team. Multiplication tables, simple addition, and subtraction problems can be answered in this manner.

For: Normal children 8 and older, retarded children in teens, handicapped children as intellectually and physically capable.

Game 59
Progressive
Addition

Equipment: Grid containing number squares.

Method: Child jumps from one number to the other. An observing child or the jumping child progressively adds the number jumped to the previous total. The observing child then takes the jumper's role.

Modifications: The jumping child can compete with the observing child to see which can reach a total first at each jump and then an overall total after ten or more jumps. A child at the blackboard, writing the same numbers, can compete with the observing child and with the jumping child to see who can add most accurately and quickly.

For: Normal children 6 and older, retarded children 8 and older, handicapped children with modifications.

Game 60
Problems
and
Answers

Equipment: Blackboard, at least two grids containing squares with numbers and operations signs ($-$, $\times$, $+$, $=$, $\div$).

Method: A child on one grid jumps out a problem, and a child on the second grid jumps the answer. Then they reverse roles. This procedure alternates with observing children checking accuracy. An inaccurate answer can change a jumper to an observer role.

Modifications: Other children can observe and record answers on blackboards adjacent to grids.

Children can remain in one operation (i.e., multiplication tables) or can constantly change operations.

For: Normal children 7 and older, retarded children in their teens, handicapped children as capable.

Equipment: TV set, basketball game, clipboards, score cards.

Method: Records of basketball players' shots are taken. Shots made from the field or the free-throw line can be collected and percentages of success computed (i.e., dividing total shots taken into number made). An actual game or a TV game can be scored.

Modifications: Team percentages of each type of shot can be recorded. Shot charts can indicate from where on court shots are taken and percentages of shots successful at various distances from the basket. Compare the percentages of losing to winning teams.

For: Normal children in late childhood or early teens, handicapped children of same ages.

**Game 61
Percentage
Basketball**

Equipment: Two stopwatches, track meet (televised or visited), clipboards, score cards.

Method: Clock the total relay time and divide by the number of legs run. Compare with actual clockings of these legs. Compare the total time of longer races (one-half mile and over) with number obtained, dividing total time by number of laps. Compare to actual lap times, clocked to the nearest tenth of a second. Compare winning times, to second- and third-place times in various races. Compute percentage differences and actual differences.

Modifications: Use bar graphs to compare lap times of individuals, of relay racers, and of first-, second-, and third-place finishers.

**Game 62
Track
Division**

For: Normal children in late childhood and teens, handicapped children of same ages.

**Game 63
Finding
Out
About
Football**

Equipment: Clipboards, score cards, football game (actual or televised).

Method: Compute yardage gained by two teams (passing versus running). Divide by the number of plays run to see the yards per play of each type. Compute the same data for individual players. Each observing child may have a different player to score. Compute the yardage gained by pass catchers, after catching passes, and because of distance pass travels. Compute kicking distances and average per kick.

Modifications: Graph the results, comparing critical differences in losing versus winning team. Score the times each team lost the ball. Compare statistics obtained by quarter;

compare these data to the scores by quarter.

For: Normal children in late childhood and early teens, handicapped children.

Summary

Although it is obvious that virtually any mathematical operation can be incorporated in some kind of movement game, the tasks described on the previous pages have been confined to basic mathematical operations: addition, subtraction, multiplication, and division. With the aid of number squares containing mathematical signs, these operations can be made more concrete for children. Various traditional games and athletic contests, such as basketball and track, have been employed to illustrate how mathematics and motivating physical activities can be combined in various ways.

Chapter 7

Letters

Practice in letter recognition may accompany games involving serial memory ability and may lead out of practice in recognizing and naming the various geometric figures. Some children, with the aid of an alphabet book read by their parents, begin to recognize and to name the letters of the alphabet by the end of their third year or the beginning of their fourth year. By the end of the fourth year, normal children can often recite the letters of the alphabet. Some children by five can block-print their first name but usually reverse letters.

These early efforts at letter recognition and naming often lack comprehension. The alphabet may be only a sing-song rhyme with little sense attached to it. The younger child may only be able to recognize and name those letters appearing in his storybook and only when the proper page is turned. In his fourth year and fifth year he probably cannot name letters correctly when they appear in a variety of type forms, and many of the letters of the alphabet may still escape his comprehension.

The games in this chapter have been subjected to a good deal of experimentation and it has been found that they do indeed help children to recognize letters visually, to write them, to name them verbally, and to identify them in a variety of forms. Letter reversal becomes less frequent after playing these games.

In a study completed in 1970 it was found that more than 70 percent of slow learners exposed to these games during a school semester for three half-hour periods a week learned the alphabet perfectly; only 30 percent of a control group given extra tutoring using traditional desk-top methods in small groups for the same period of time posted perfect scores. Findings from other investigations have been equally encouraging.

On inspecting these games, it will become apparent that the number of activities "getting at" letter recognition is indeed endless. The games represent large categories of activities whose expansion is limited only by the imaginations of the teachers and of the children.

I have attempted to incorporate in the games activities that enable children to hear, see, move, and name the letters of the alphabet with all possible combinations of sensory experiences employed (i.e., see and move, hear and write, jump and write). Games involving this type of intersensory integration include Games 64, 65, 70, and 72.

Furthermore, it is important for children to be exposed to upper-case and lower-case letters, large and small letters, and letters written in manuscript form. Not until the age of seven or eight can most normal children engage in all the possible matchings of letter types, and later in life they are often confused when a new type form is viewed. Games 74 and 75 exemplify the type of activity that should take place to facilitate this type of intercategory integration of various forms of a single letter.

To a child at the age of four, a spoon is a spoon—whether it is hanging on a wall, lying on the floor, or resting on the table. However, as he reaches his fifth and sixth years society lets him know that somehow curious letter shapes must somehow be viewed, written, and read, within a constant left-right, up-down reference system. The child finds, sometimes to his surprise, that adults do not give their approval to his efforts when he writes an *E* backward; similar censure is awarded him when he reverses other letters of the alphabet.

Thus practice in letter recognition should be accompanied by parallel and near-simultaneous efforts to write the same letter on a blackboard or table. Stress at this point should be placed on just which way, for example, the open part of the block *C* faces or on which side the long straight part of the *F* comes. A variety of left-right and up-down games may aid the child to better perceive these spatial relationships. If direct transfer is taught for two letter shapes (i.e., "See, John, the open part of the *E* faces toward your right hand"), letter reversal problems may be corrected.[1]

Letters may be reversed, however, and the child may read well. At the same time, the order of letters in words may be reversed (i.e., *no* instead of *on*) and the letters themselves may be either correctly printed or reversed. Thus the problem is extremely complex. More about this problem will be discussed in Chapter 8.

Most of the games in this chapter involve some use of the blackboard. Placing letters on a playground, in whatever form, will not aid letter recognition unless specific lessons are taught and integrated with classroom activities and correct sequences are followed. Letters should be taught with their accompanying sounds, and this procedure naturally leads into spelling and reading. Many of the games in this chapter, including Games 72 through 75, lead toward this type of progression.

As in games found in the other chapters, it has often been attempted to indicate just how a child's auditory and/or visual memory may be enhanced. A letter may be written or spoken in several of the games (such as Games 64 and 65), and then a time delay may be allowed before the child

---

[1] In one study by my colleagues and me, a "location" score evidenced by a group of children was significantly raised after five months of various games in which spatial coordinates were stressed. The score was obtained from a drawing test in which various geometric figures had to be drawn in the proper corners of a larger square drawn first.

is permitted to make the overt movement response inherent in the game. It is believed that the type of subvocal rehearsal that he will usually have to engage in, or the process of visual imagery that he may have to evoke during this time period, is a helpful perceptual-cognitive exercise.

Also, as in other games in the book, modifications may be made to accommodate handicapped children. Even children confined to wheelchairs enjoy throwing bean bags or other missiles in order to participate in the tasks outlined.

Equipment: Blackboard, letter squares, chalk.
Method: Child observes block letter printed on board and from two choices attempts to indicate correct match by jumping in the appropriate letter square. The board is erased, another letter is written, and a choice is made from two or three squares.
Modifications: Increase the number of squares from three up to twenty-six. Vary the response requested (i.e., hop, jump around, run around). The handicapped child may throw a bean bag into the squares of his

**Game 64
Match
and
Jump**

choice. Another child may act as teacher, writing a letter or number on the board, while a third child may observe and correct the jumper. The game becomes more difficult if the letter is written and then erased prior to eliciting a response from the child.

For: Normal children 3–7 years, retarded children 6–16 years, handicapped children of all ages with modifications outlined.

**Game 65
Tell,
Find,
and
Tell**

Equipment: Letter and number squares.

Method: The child is told a letter verbally. He must then find it from two or more choices, jump in it, and at the same time repeat verbally the name of the letter. More than one letter at a time can be called prior to eliciting more than one jump.

Modifications: The child must choose from among an increasing number of choices. Increase the period of time allowed to elapse between telling by teacher (or another child) and the responses made by the learner (jumping and telling again). A chain-reaction game may be played as a child jumps and tells after being told and then in turn jumps and tells on another letter, which must be repeated by a third child, then a fourth child, etc.

For: Normal children 4–7 years, retarded children 6–16 years, handicapped children with modifications.

**Game 66
Find
Them**

Equipment: Blackboard, lined configurations using painted lines or lining tape as shown.

Method: Letters are placed on the blackboard, one at a time. Students are required to find them in the complex configurations and confirm them by running through the shapes.

Modifications: Students may first write them again. Before running, they may hop or skip through configurations. Observing students can check on accuracy. Running through a letter or number may precede writing it on the board.

For: Normal children 5–10 years, retarded children 7–15 years.

Equipment: Sandbox, blackboard.

Method: Write a letter (or tell it), and then ask the child to walk through its shape in the sandbox. An observing child can correct errors. The walking child can see his own footprints. He must wipe the sand level after walking to ensure inspection of subsequent footprints.

Modifications: The teacher may start with simple geometric patterns and gradually progress to letter shapes. The child may first inspect numbers and letters in a horizontal plane before walking them in the same plane. The transposition from a vertical plane (blackboard) to a horizontal plane (sandbox) can cause problems.

For: Normal children 4–8 years, retarded children 6–16 years.

Game 68
Playground
Letters

Equipment: Blackboard or clipboards containing paper, playground (unmarked).

Method: After showing a child a simple geometric figure or letter shape, ask him to run or walk through its configurations on the playground. Ask an observing child to check accuracy. (Note: Footprints will not leave marks as in Game 67.)

Modifications: A child may be asked to run through a series of letters or a whole sentence. This type of task is an extremely difficult undertaking.

For: Normal children 6–8 years, retarded children 10–15 years.

Game 69
Alphabet
Games

Equipment: Letter squares.

Method: Children, one at a time, may select from the letters those that belong in order in the alphabet. The letters may be arranged in order and talked about as the children hop or jump on them.

Modifications: Letters may be lower-case or upper-case. They may be jumped on backward or forward, from the *A* or from the *Z* in the alphabet. Relays may be run to see which team can construct a line of letter squares forming the alphabet first. A teacher or student "caller" can call the correct letters in order, to which responding children can react by selecting appropriate letter squares and arranging them in the proper order.

For: Normal children 3–6 years, retarded children 6–15 years.

Equipment: Blackboard, letter squares arranged in grid and placed together as shown.

**Game 70
Letter
Hopscotch**

G	F	U	B	V	K
O	Y	N	S	D	L
U	A	I	Q	E	O
T	Y	Z		R	X
D	W	M	C	B	I
P	J	E	A	H	S

Method: One or more children can attempt to respond quickly to letters, written one at a time on the board or given orally one at a time, by jumping into the corresponding square on the grid as shown.

Modifications: Children can hop, compete with one another, or work alone. Children can call letters aloud to themselves as they jump from letter to letter in a single row (thus six children can work at a time). After jumping in correct letter, given orally, the child can be asked to copy it on the board. Letter locations should be changed frequently to avoid recognition by location rather than shape.

For: Normal children 4–8 years, retarded children 7–16 years, handicapped children (using throwing tasks) at any age depending on mental abilities.

Equipment: Blackboard, score sheets, squares containing letters.

Method: One child at a time from each of two teams should be asked to go to a group of letters, run back with one, place it in order, and tag the next member of his team. Repeat until the entire series of letters (the alphabet) is placed side by side. The winning team is the one that completes the series first.

Modifications: Children in wheelchairs can be wheeled for letters. Normal children can be encouraged to use a variety of movement patterns, such as hopping, skipping, etc.

For: Normal children 3–6 years, retarded children 7–16 years, handicapped children of various ages depending on mental capacity.

**Game 71
Letter
Relays**

87

**Game 72
Cutting,
Looking,
and
Finding**

Equipment: Paper, scissors, letter squares, blackboard.

Method: Have the child cut out a letter, find it on the letter grid, jump in it, and draw it on the blackboard. The child then cuts out two or more letters, holds them in his hand while he jumps into their corresponding letter on the grid, and shuffles a new letter to the top of the pack after each jump.

Modifications: For some groups of children (i.e., retarded) a single letter may be a project for a single day (or week). They must find out all about the letter in all its forms by cutting, touching, drawing, looking, and finding it on the grids.

For: Normal children 3–7 years, retarded children 6–16 years, handicapped children as capable.

**Game 73
Flash
and
Jump**

Equipment: Flash cards containing numbers, letter squares to jump in.

Method: Letters are flashed briefly, one at a time. The child must then recognize the letter and jump in the appropriate letter match on the larger squares.

Modifications: Two children may compete, first observing the flash card and then attempting to jump first into the appropriate matching squares. Both upper-case and lower-case letters may be used (i.e., flash lower-case and jump in upper-case letters). Handicapped children may throw bean bags into appropriate squares.

For: Normal children 3–7 years, retarded children 6–16 years, handicapped children with modifications.

**Game 74
Upper-Case,
Lower-Case**

Equipment: Flash cards, letter squares containing both lower- and upper-case letters in separate squares.

Method: The child may be given a packet of flash cards containing lower-case letters to hold.

Observing them one at a time in his hand, he tries to jump in the appropriate upper-case letter on the larger squares. The teacher may flash upper-case letters and have the child attempt, by himself or in competition with another child, to jump in corresponding lower-case letters.

Modifications: A handicapped child may throw bean bags into appropriate squares. Matching may also be done solely in larger squares (i.e., a child may first jump into an upper-case letter and then find the corresponding lower-case letter and hop in it). A "student teacher" may show a group of two or three children an upper-case letter by jumping into it, and then the other children can compete to see who can jump first into the corresponding lower-case letter.

For: Normal children 5–8 years, retardates 7–15 years, handicapped children as capable.

89

**Game 75
Script,
Printing**

Equipment: Blackboard, letter squares containing lower- and upper-case letters.

Method: Letters may be written one at a time on the board in script, and then the child must find the upper-case and lower-case printed equivalent on the appropriate squares by jumping in them, hopping in them, etc.

Modifications: Children may compete in this manner after observing manuscript letters. Increasing periods of time may elapse after a letter is written, and it may be erased prior to permitting a movement response.

For: Normal children 7–10 years, retardates 8–15 years, handicapped children as capable intellectually.

Summary

The tasks involving letter recognition outlined in this chapter have approached this skill from several standpoints. Children are encouraged to translate letter shapes of various kinds (block-printing, lower-case, script) into their verbal as well as their written equivalents. The final portions of the chapter contain games that lead into those in the following chapter, which deals with letter sounds and spelling.

Research by others has shown that facility in letter recognition is predictive of reading success. Furthermore, groups of poor and good readers are readily distinguished by comparing their abilities to discern letter shapes and letter sounds.

Chapter 8

Letter Sounds and Spelling

The English language is difficult to learn. The same letters have different sounds in various words. Children have the same difficulty straightening these sounds out and matching them with appropriate letters and letter combinations as do foreigners confronted with our language later in life.

The games in this chapter are attempts to make the difficult process of translating letter shapes into sounds, and sounds and letters into words, a little more palatable and a little less oppressive. Spelling is not reading, and often a child will read reasonably well while remaining an average or below-average speller. Children read by attaching meaning to word shapes. They often use cues within the context of a sentence, or the shape of the first letter, or other cues independent of the spelling of the word to decide on its sound and meaning.

The games are not meant to be exhaustive; they are only indicative of several types that may be utilized to advantage. We need not have limited ourselves to only seventeen games—there are perhaps 1700 we might have devised if our space permitted. The children will probably demonstrate modifications that *they* think of, which will help the teacher to discover the vast range of possibilities.

Traditionally, each week in schools throughout the United States teachers submit to their children a list of ten words to learn to spell. The children study the list, and usually on Wednesday night they must place the words into sentences. Of course on Friday they take the spelling test. On Monday the results are given back, and the process is repeated the following week. Some of the games in this chapter may make this weekly routine more palatable to the children and, as a result, more fun for the teacher. What about some spelling games on Tuesday?

As in the other game series in this book, I have attempted to employ all the facilities of the learners and to combine them to various degrees. In some games the children practice listening for words or for the spelling of words before they respond in the form of a movement. In others they may write their responses or write the word to be spelled. As in the games involving serial memory and letter recognition, visual and auditory memory is exercised. Some of the games may be modified to permit an interval between the time the problem is presented visually or orally and the time the child is required to respond in some way. This time interval, during which mental rehearsal of the letters takes place involving subvocalizations or visual imagery, may indeed be the most helpful part of the games.

Some of the games involve the child's responding by moving to the appropriate letters, and in others the child must collect the letters and move *them* in some way. Additionally, and unlike most classroom drills in spelling, many of the words dealt with are spelled one letter at a time, via jumping or other movements, and thus do not give the child the opportunity to observe the previous and subsequent letters of the word. This type of exercise is probably more difficult for most children than the usual types of spelling drills employed in the class.

Several of the games are indeed vocabulary games rather than spelling games and thus bridge the gap between spelling and reading. Games 89 and 90 are examples of these. Other tasks require the child to carry out movement responses to a verbal or printed direction. (Games of this type are also found in Chapter 9.) These types of activities are predicated on the supposition made by many language authorities that the infant's first speech patterns and recognition of words take place as he is responding to some directions involving movement ("Come here," "Don't do that," "Stop," "Bring that here," "Let's see you stand" . . . "walk"). Game 88 is an example of this type.

Some of the games may be employed directly in activities involving creative writing, vocabulary drill, and other common English exercises. Games 86 and 92 represent this type.

Additionally, some of the games require the child to write letters in order on a blackboard. No attempt is made to divorce games of letter recognition, spelling, and the like from writing the letters and words; it is believed helpful to combine these operations in the ways indicated in Game 91.

There are several sample games in which phonics teaching is combined with movements of various kinds. This technique is not necessarily a commitment to the phonics method of teaching, but those so committed can modify and expand these games to suit their own needs and to correspond closely to a phonics approach to spelling and reading. In my experience, attempting to teach spelling without sounding out letters and letter combinations is less than fruitful.

Although spelling is not necessarily directly related to reading, many children who spell well also read well. Furthermore, spelling *is* an integral part of the ability to communicate effectively in writing. During the 1930s and 1940s great emphasis in the schools was placed on sight reading, which required children to depend primarily on word shapes for recognition. It was later found that a generation of poor spellers was produced. In the 1950s and 1960s educators and parents concerned with this apparent type of illiteracy seen in children from previous generations attempted to instill increased emphasis on spelling in the schools. Hopefully the activities in this chapter will make their efforts more fruitful.

My research has indicated that improvement in spelling is more pronounced when children are exposed to games of this nature than when they are given additional small-group practice in the classroom. Thus it is with some confidence that I outline these games.

Game 76
Shown
and
Sound

Equipment: Letter squares and blackboard as shown.

Method: Using a blackboard, print hard consonants (*D, B, C, T, K, P,* etc.) and have the child find them on letter grid by jumping in them. Conversely, the child can, using the grid containing hard consonants, jump in each and sound out their hard sound (i.e., jump in *B* and say "*B* as in *boy,*" jump in *C* and say "*C* as in *cut*").

Modifications: Teacher or teaching student can say hard consonant sounds, and the child can find the appropriate grid letter and hop in it, jump in it, etc. The handicapped child can throw a bean bag in the appropriate squares.

For: Normal children 6–8 years, retarded children 8–16 years, handicapped (with throwing modification) of all ages.

Game 77
Vowel
Sounds

Equipment: Letter squares, blackboard. Arrange vowels as shown.

Method: First make sure the child knows the vowels by name. Then place various vowels on the board, indicating how each should be pronounced by proper accent marks over words (i.e., *ä* or *ā*, *ē*). The child finds the proper letter in grid squares and confirms his knowledge by jumping or hopping in it.

Modifications: With more advanced children, pronounce the word with the vowel sound and then ask the child to write the vowel sound and to find the vowel by jumping in it, hopping in it, etc.

For: Normal children 7–12 years, retarded children (educable) 8–15 years, handicapped children of all ages.

Equipment: Blackboard, letter squares containing consonants whose sounds are relatively consistent (as shown).

W	J	V	Z
B	M	N	F
V	Y	Z	S
D	F	T	R

Method: The child tells the sound and finds it in the grid by jumping, etc. Conversely, he may jump in the grid and pronounce the sound on arriving there.

Modifications: The child can find sounds within words, make up words having these sounds, and jump them out (correct letters in order, etc.). Handicapped children can "answer" by throwing bean bags, etc.

For: Normal children 6–12 years, retarded children 7–15 years, handicapped children.

**Game 79
Spelling:
See,
Hear,
and
Spell**

Equipment: Blackboard, letter squares, twenty-six letters placed in grid.

Method: Spell word verbally and write it out on the blackboard. While it remains, the child duplicates the word by jumping in the proper squares in order on the grid.

Modifications: Spell short words verbally only. Write the word but then erase it. The child must duplicate it by jumping or hopping. Two or more children, each with separate grids, attempt to spell letters as quickly as possible in competition. An observing child for each confirms accuracy.

For: Normal children 5–12 years, retarded children 7–15 years, handicapped children (throwing bean bags to confirm letter choice).

**Game 80
Anagrams**

Equipment: Five or more letter squares per child, with each set of five containing at least one vowel.

Method: Each child must jump through as many words as he can with his set of letters. This task becomes increasingly easy as the number of letters allotted each child is increased. Each jumping child should have an observing child counting words and making sure of accurate spelling. Using a grid of thirty-six squares (six feet by six feet), six students, each with a row, can play at the same time.

Modifications: Set time limits per set of five words, and then add two letters every two minutes, etc.

For: Normal children 6–12 years, retarded children 8–16 years, handicapped children of all ages.

Equipment: Pencils and paper; nine, sixteen, twenty-five, or thirty-six letter grids.

Method: Divide the children into teams of three or four members each. Each team, using their grid, thinks of as many words as possible. One member records, a second observes spelling, and a third jumps through the word being added to the list. At the end of a time period, lists are compared for number of words and accuracy of spelling.

Modifications: Rotate observers, recorders, and jumpers.

For: Normal children 6–12 years, retarded children 7–15 years, handicapped children of all ages.

**Game 81
Team
Spelling**

Equipment: Blackboard, letter squares.

Method: Place all letters (several alphabets) together. With two teams of players, place a reasonably long word on the blackboard to spell via a relay. One player from each team runs to get the first letter, returns, and tags a second, who returns with the second, places it next to the first, and in

**Game 82
Spelling
Relays**

this way spells the entire word. The first team completed wins.

Modifications: For handicapped children, two teams may be formed of children in wheelchairs. One at a time they may be pushed to a letter grid, throw a bean bag with a string attached at the appropriate letter, in order, and then return to have the second child pushed to the grid.

For: Normal children 7–12 years, retarded children 8–16 years, handicapped children of all ages.

**Game 83
Running
Spelling
Games**

Equipment: Blackboard, lined area containing patterns (as shown) made with lining tape or permanent yellow painted lines.

Method: Using one or two teams, individuals try (against a stopwatch or in competition

with one another) to run through all the
letters in a given order, using the grids as
shown. The word is placed on the blackboard.

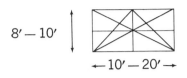 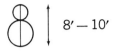

Modifications: The children can use a sandbox, without
marked lines. They may skip, hop, or
jump through the letters.
For: Normal children 7–12 years, retarded children 9–16 years.

Equipment: Letter squares.
Method: A word is given aloud, and the child tries
to spell it on the grid containing letter
squares by jumping, etc., into the appropriate squares.
Modifications: Two children may compete on the same
or on different grids to see how fast each
can complete the word by jumping or
hopping into squares. Words may be
spelled by throwing bean bags.
For: Normal children 7–12 years, retarded
children 8–15 years, handicapped children as capable.

**Game 84
Hear
and
Spell**

Equipment: Blackboard, letter squares forming one or
more grids.
Method: One member at a time from each of two
teams attempts as fast as possible to spell
words given orally. The opposite team
observes for accuracy. The winning team
finishes first after each member has
spelled one word.
Modifications: After jumping or hopping out the word, the
child may write it on the blackboard. Chil-

**Game 85
Hearing
and
Spelling
Relays**

dren in wheelchairs may be pushed one
at a time to the grid, into which they may
throw bean bags to spell words.

For: Normal children 7–12 years, retarded children 8–15 years, handicapped children as
capable.

**Game 86
Spell
a
Story**

Equipment: Letter squares.

Method: Two or more children alternately "tell" a
story by jumping words in the grid. One
child starts with a word; the next child
continues the story by a second word, etc.,
until a story is "told."

Modifications: The story may be a familiar one, but it
should be made up by the children. The
usual modifications may be made for children who cannot jump or hop.

For: Normal children 8–15 years, retarded children 10–15 years, handicapped children
as capable.

**Game 87
Same
or
Opposite**

Equipment: Blackboard, letter squares placed in grids
or in lines.

Method: A word is spelled on the blackboard, and
the child must then jump in the grid a
word that is the same or opposite.

Modifications: The first word can be given orally or
jumped on the grid, and the second word
can be jumped or thrown via bean bags.

For: Normal children 8–15 years, retarded children 10–15 years, handicapped children
as capable.

**Game 88
Spell
It
and
Do
It**

Equipment: Blackboard containing letters.

Method: The first child spells a verb by jumping,
throwing, hopping, etc., into appropriate
squares on the grid (i.e., "jump," "skip").
The second child indicates his understand-

ing by performing the action. The second child, if correct, can instruct the first child or a third child in the same manner. Instructions can be a single word ("run") or a phrase ("pick up the pencil").

Modifications: Instructions can be more subtle ("Spell another word for *sorry*") as well as simple verb or verb phrases. Groups of children can perform for one "teacher," who jumps directions.

For: Normal children 6–12 years, retarded children 8–15 years, handicapped children as capable.

Equipment: Blackboard, letter squares.

Method: The child is asked to spell, via jumping in squares, etc., a word that sounds the same but has a different meaning from the one placed on the blackboard or spelled out for him and pronounced (i.e., *bear, bare*).

Modifications: The child can be asked to think up pairs of words himself. One child can think up a word, and a second can think of a matching word.

For: Normal children 8–14 years, handicapped children as intellectually capable.

Game 89
The
Same
But
Different

Equipment: Blackboard, letter squares.

Method: A word is placed on the blackboard, and the child jumps its definition in squares. Or, the child is given the definition and then spells the answer by jumping into the proper squares in order.

Modifications: Words or definitions may be given orally rather than written on the board. Handicapped children can give answers by throwing bean bags.

For: Normal children 8–16 years, retarded children 10–16 years, handicapped children as capable intellectually.

Game 90
Definitions

**Game 91
Writing
and
Printing**

Equipment: Letter squares, blackboard.

Method: A word is written on the board, and the child must jump appropriate letters in order on the larger squares. Writing is made in manuscript, but response is on printed letters, both upper- and lower-case.

Modifications: Manuscript letters on larger blocks may be obtained, and the child must find corresponding letters on other blocks containing printed letters (that is, first jump into one type of letter while spelling a word and then jump into the same letters in the other style (i.e., manuscript). Proper names requiring upper-case letters should be used at times.

For: Normal children 8–12 years, retarded children 10–15 years, handicapped children as capable.

Equipment: Letter squares arranged in large circles.

Method: Children walk around a circle outside letters to music. They stop beside the nearest letter when the music stops, and they tell the name of the letter and make a word starting with that letter. Each time a letter is removed, so that there will be one fewer letter than children. The child left out each time is out of the game.

Modifications: The word to be thought of can be within a different announced category each time (i.e., fruit, country, occupation). Words can also be used in a sentence.

For: Normal children 7 and over, retarded children (educables) in their teens, handicapped children with obvious modifications.

Summary

This chapter provides a variety of spelling games. Additionally, activities intended to aid children to translate letter shapes and letter combinations into the variety of sounds that they are likely to assume in the English language are also described. As in all the chapters, the tasks are presented in the approximate order of difficulty. A more comprehensive program of phonics games may be devised with the aid of any of the available handbooks dealing with this method of teaching spelling and reading. For example, the Open Court Method was utilized in much of my research.

Chapter 9

Reading

Reading is a complex and often misunderstood act. Some theorists have suggested that reading is closely related to the facility with which a child can move his eyes; others have stated that reading is a process that can be enhanced by having children walk balance beams and otherwise improve their general coordination. In innumerable studies I have reviewed elsewhere, these rather simplistic assertions are found to be less than valid.[1]

Rather, it is believed that reading is largely a cognitive act. Children must certainly look at a word when they try to read it, and thus their visual apparatus must be reasonably well intact; but they must also be able to attach a

---

[1] See the chapter reviewing data exploring various perceptual-motor theories in Bryant J. Cratty, *Perceptual and Motor Development of Infants and Children* (New York: The Macmillan Company, Publishers, 1970).

thought to the word shape they view. Furthermore, they must often say the word that the letter-configuration shape suggests.

The findings from study after study during the past twenty years have indicated that practice in reading is the most likely method of improving reading. Walking balance beams is likely to improve the important quality of balance but little else.

It was on these basic premises that the games in this chapter were devised and researched. The results from my studies have been promising indeed. However, these games do not constitute a total reading program but are most helpful when used as motivating practice sessions interposed at appropriate times throughout the school week.

In some games sight reading and verbalizing have been accompanied by the need to define a word, to place it into a sentence, or to otherwise deal with it. In this way the child forms more associations between the word shape and the meaning and sound of the word.

Many of the tasks involve sight reading, which in turn leads to some progression in a game entirely removed from the word itself. Game 101 is of this type. Other games require a child to follow directions, after either making up these directions or getting them in some form from another child. Some of the final games in the series require this type of activity on the part of the children.

Most of the games permit teams of children to work with one another in various ways. Children can act as "observers," checking on the accuracy of other children who may serve as initiating "teachers" and of others who function as "students." In this way larger groups can be worked with, and the children can begin to take over an increasing number of decisions from the teacher when they prove able to do so.

Some of the games, particularly when the children attempt to match words with things and to carry out actions in response to simple directions, are obviously limited primarily to the reading of verbs and nouns. Other games in the series, however, are more expansive in their influence on word recognition and require the integration of a variety of parts of speech into sentences and the gaining of meaning from written, printed, and oral directions.

As is generally true in this text, the games in this chapter require an obvious observable response on the part of the child—a response whose quality can easily be assessed by the teacher, both for accuracy and speed. Another common principle underlying these activities is that a number of sensory modalities may be incorporated into each activity. Children are taught to listen, to write words, to act out directions, and in similar ways to obtain a wide variety of experiences in connection with a single word or phrase.

These reading games pose no educational cure-all for the reading problems of children. However, my studies have indicated that they offer highly motivating exercises that tend to benefit many active children more than does additional exposure to reading drills in a more passive context.

**Game 93
See
and
Jump**

Equipment: Flash cards containing pictures, squares containing printed words.

Method: Card, containing noun, is flashed. The child jumps into the appropriate noun on the square in front of him. Start with two possible squares, and then gradually increase the number of choices.

Modifications: Other responses can be used, such as: hopping or skipping. The noun can be spoken (i.e., *boy, girl, ball*) and then the proper square jumped in.

For: Normal children 5 and older, retarded children 7 and older, handicapped children (by throwing bean bags).

Equipment: Blackboard, squares containing printed words, lettered squares.

Method: One child can draw picture of something (i.e., girl) on the board, and an observing child can then find the corresponding word shape. He jumps into the square containing the word shape and/or jumps through the correct letters, in order, in the letter grid.

Modifications: Competition can be introduced between two or more children observing the drawing.

For: Normal children 6 and older, retarded children 8 and older, handicapped children.

**Game 94
Draw
and
Hop**

**Game 95
Hop
and
Say**

Equipment: Letter squares, flash cards containing pictures, and large jumping squares containing pictures of persons, places, and things.

Method: The child is given a name verbally (i.e., *boy*). He must find it in squares containing words, jump in it, and then jump in the correct letters in order on the letter grid.

Modifications: A flash card containing pictures can be shown to the child, and then he may respond by hopping or jumping into appropriate squares.

For: Normal children 5 and older, retarded children 7 and older, handicapped children.

**Game 96
Steal
the
Word**

Equipment: Words on large squares placed between two teams.

Method: Children on each team are given numbers starting with 1. A number is called, to-

gether with a word. A child from each team attempts to retrieve the word called from the middle of the teams. The winner gets a point. The teacher should call "house-2" rather than "2-house" so all children think about the word.

Modifications: The word can be flashed and its match sought by each pair of children called.

For: Normal children 6 and older, retarded children 7 and older, handicapped children (with modifications).

Game 97
Story
Relays

Equipment: Blackboard, chalk.

Method: Choose two teams of ten or more children each. The first child on each team runs to the blackboard, begins a sentence, returns, tags the next child in order, and each child adds a word until all members are finished. They must form a coherent sentence or sentences. The first team finished wins.

Modifications: Children may race, using movements other than running. Sentences may be formed from cards containing words, rather than written on the blackboard one word at a time.

For: Normal children 7 and older, retarded children 8 and older, handicapped children (with modifications).

Game 98
Read
and
Act

Equipment: Blackboard; flash cards containing verbs or verb phrases; letter, word, or number squares; balls.

Method: A card is flashed, and the child must act out the verb. An observing child checks the appropriate nature of the movement (i.e., run, jump, draw a circle, jump in a "cat," hop in an *A*). If the child is correct, he may become a teacher, drawing a new card. The child previously flashing the card becomes the performer. The procedure may be used with groups of three or more children—one a card flasher, the second an observer-scorer, and the third performing the movement.

Modifications: Competition may be set up between teams of children. Correct or incorrect scores determine the total team score. The game can start with an act (i.e., running) and then an attempt can be made to find the appropriate word.

For: Normal children 7 and older, retarded children 8 and older, handicapped children of all ages (with modifications).

Game 99
Reading
Directions

Equipment: Number, letter, and word squares, cards containing a series of directions (i.e., run, jump, walk into a square).

Method: A child is given a card and a set period of time to read the directions. An observing child then takes the card and determines whether the first child is carrying out the directions in the correct order and appropriately.

Modifications: Four, five, or more directions can be given. Activities required can become progressively more difficult. Competition between two or more children, following the same or different directions, can be introduced, with the winner determined by accuracy and/or speed.

For: Normal children 8 and older, retarded children 10 and older, handicapped children (with modifications) as capable.

Game 100 Matching Words

Equipment: Flash cards containing words, squares containing their match (i.e., the same sound with a different meaning and spelling), letter squares.

Method: Children must observe the flash card and then jump in, retrieve, or spell out a word that sounds the same but is different (i.e., *bear, bare*; *reed, read*).

Modifications: Words can be spoken in a sentence, either when presented or when matched. The words can be spoken singly and both alternatives (or three alternatives) spelled out.

For: Normal children 8 and older, educable retardates in their teens, handicapped children as capable.

Game 101 Base Progress

Equipment: Cards containing vocabulary words, a three- or four-base game facility.

Method: Two teams alternate. The hitter on the up team must name the word flashed by a member of the other team. If he does, he may go to first base; if not, he is out (after five outs the other team is up). Members of the up team force one another around the bases and score runs when forced home. The fielding team selects harder words to flash (or write on a board) as the game progresses.

Modifications: Children may run, hop, or otherwise negotiate the bases. Words flashed may indi-

cate how a child may proceed from base to base (run, skip, walk, etc., giving help in verb recognition).

For: Normal children 7 and older, retarded children 8 and older, handicapped children (with modifications).

**Game 102
Reading
Basketball**

Equipment: Basketball hoop, balls, blackboard and/or flash cards containing vocabulary words.

Method: Two teams, each at a different basket, must name the words flashed (or written on the board) by a member of opposite team. If this is done, the team member gets to attempt a basket (point is scored if word is named correctly, and a second point is scored if the basket attempt is successful).

Modifications: Children who make a basket can move from spot to spot around the court to earn additional points. If only one basket is available, the children can have an up

team and a flashing (or writing) team.
Shooting can be preceded by dribbling the
ball.

For: Normal children 7 and older, retarded children 9 and older, handicapped children of
all ages (with ability to shoot baskets).

Equipment: Footballs, blackboard or flash cards of vocabulary words to be learned, tape mea-
sures, playground balls, softballs, bean
bags.

Method: Each child coming "up" is given a word
(via a flash card or written on the blackboard). He must name it correctly, use it
in a sentence, and then throw the football
for distance. Points are scored according
to distance thrown, whether word is cor-

**Game 103
Read,
Pass,
or
Throw**

rectly pronounced, and whether it is used in a sentence correctly. Points for throwing distance depend on age and ability level of the children.

Modifications: Children flashing cards or drawing words on the board check accuracy and may take the throwers' places if they are incorrect. Balls of various types may be thrown corresponding to ability, sex, physical disability, etc. Balls may be batted or kicked for distance, rather than thrown.

For: Normal children 7 and older, retarded children 8 and older, handicapped children (with modifications).

**Game 104
Obstacle
Course
Reading**

Equipment: Tires, boxes, mats, tape, ropes, hoops.
Method: A child may proceed through an obstacle course if he is able to read a new word placed on each obstacle. After each run-through new words are placed on the obstacles. Team or individual competition can be introduced. Additional points for

finishing time and/or the ability to use a word in a sentence can be given.

Modifications: The obstacle course may be made with lining tape, using two-dimensional obstacles rather than more elaborate three-dimensional obstacles. Children in wheelchairs may have "obstacles" in the form of things to throw bean bags into or over (scrap baskets, circles on the floor).

For: Normal children 6 and older, retarded children 8 and older, handicapped children (with modifications).

Game 105 Write a Story

Equipment: Paper and pencil, equipment as needed.

Method: Classroom time is devoted to the assignment of writing a movement story. Playground time is then devoted to reading the story by other class members and carrying out activities as it is read.

Modifications: Reading may be done aloud accompanying movements. Stories may be reasonably complex and need not include the need for constant movement. A child may read the story silently and act out movements as needed.

For: Normal children 8 and older, handicapped children as capable.

Game 106 Wait and Read

Equipment: Blackboard, flash cards containing words.

Method: One member at a time from two relay teams is required to read a word flashed (or written on a board). If he can, he may leave immediately on his relay trip; if not, he must delay one, two, or three seconds before starting. The trip can consist of dodging, running, etc. He returns to tap the next person, who is then shown the next word.

Modifications: If the word meaning can be supplied by the next team member in line, the starting penalty time may be reduced. If the word can be pronounced but not used in a sentence, more penalty time is introduced. If the word can be used in a sentence by the second teammate, the penalty time can be reduced.

For: Normal children 8 and older, retarded children 9 and older, handicapped children (with modifications).

**Game 107
Read
and
Run**

Equipment: Room or athletic field, flash cards containing words.

Method: Place pairs of cards, each containing different words, one under the other at various stations in the room or on an athletic field. Children each start with a different "top" word and then quickly look underneath, finding the second different word, which they must then run and find as another top word. They then look underneath that third word, finding the next word to which they must run, etc.

Modifications: Individual children can be timed through the word obstacle course. Groups of children can go at once, each one trying to catch the next child. Words can be increasingly difficult. Children can be asked to make up a sentence on finding each word.

For: Normal children 7 and older, retarded children in their teens, handicapped children (with modifications).

Summary

Various motivating games that should enhance the ability of a child to read are contained in this chapter. The games have been designed not only to give a boy or girl the initial impetus to translate word shapes into word sounds (sight read) but also to aid the child to derive meaning from word shapes.

The tasks in this chapter do not represent a comprehensive method of teaching reading but merely suggest some kinds of motivating experiences that may be used in conjunction with traditional classroom reading practice.

Chapter 10

How, To Whom, With What, How Often, And Why?

By now you no doubt have many questions. For example, the classroom teacher hardened by exposure to classes too large to teach may well say, "This is fine, but what can I do with the rest of my class while one or two are hopping into squares?" The parent concerned about the learning problem of his offspring may question just how and where he can collect the necessary equipment listed for some of the games.

This chapter does not and cannot contain all the answers to questions you may have. It is impossible to see into all situations in which these games may be used and to prescribe just how various difficulties encountered may be overcome. However, in the following pages I will attempt to be as practical as possible and to outline just how these activities worked best both in research studies and in schools and clinical situations in which they have been employed. Perhaps the most important question answered in this chapter is "How shall I teach?"

Chapters 2, 3, and 4 are relatively basic to all types of classroom learning. Chapters 5 and 6 lead toward qualitative concepts and relationships underlying mathematics, and Chapters 7, 8, and 9 concern themselves with letters, spelling, reading, and verbal skills. Thus the teacher or parent may choose to try all these activities or to "branch off" into the verbal or arithmetic "channels" after considering and practicing the games. Diagramed, this relationship is as follows:

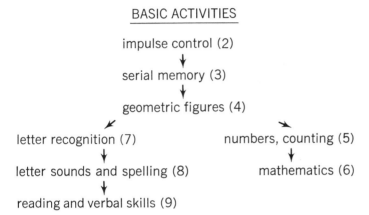

BASIC ACTIVITIES

impulse control (2)

serial memory (3)

geometric figures (4)

letter recognition (7)   numbers, counting (5)

letter sounds and spelling (8)   mathematics (6)

reading and verbal skills (9)

How Often and When?

In our research my colleagues and I have conducted learning sessions composed of these games from three to five times a week. These sessions have lasted about half an hour each and have been given in the morning hours from 9:00 to 11:30. In general the classroom teacher may schedule them from two to three times a week or as often as deemed necessary.

There is an often researched phenomenon concerning the learning of both motor and verbal skills that is often—indeed usually—overlooked in preparing curricula. It is usually found that, if practice in verbal and motor skills is placed too closely together in time, a certain amount of inhibition to the tasks will take place and the amount of progress will begin to decrease from trial to trial or from practice session to practice session. Despite this well-known fact, certain school subjects are legislated by law to be taught a given length of time daily. Hopefully, someday the curriculum designers will become more familiar with this research and begin to space practice sessions more advantageously throughout the school week, rather than adhere to some preconceived and often inaccurate law that may be at odds with well-researched principles of learning.

A good way to encourage learning on the part of children—and this is true when using the games in this text as well as when employing traditional methods—is to present interesting short lessons with reasonably long rest intervals between each so that some of the information can begin to "soak in" and less inhibition to learning occurs on the part of the children. As a corollary to this principle, it is recommended that the frequency of the practice of some of the learning games be left up to the sensitive teacher's discretion. Some weeks they may be given daily and at other times less frequently. At times, if the game really is going well, it may be extended for an hour or even more; at other times its duration may be shortened and another game introduced or the games suspended entirely.

Investigations have found that the best physical and mental performance usually occurs in children during the latter part of the morning, from 10:30 to 11:00. Some time during most school mornings a recess or physical education period occurs. It is probably best to place some kind of learning game just before such a period as a kind of thinking-movement warmup for more vigorous physical activities conducted on the playground. *These learning games were not intended nor should they be a substitute for a good program of physical education.* If they are conducted after a period of physical education, it may be necessary to spend some time with the tasks in Chapter 2 to calm the children down prior to their administration.

At home these games can be played for short periods at the end of the day. Some research concerning which teachers children learn best from indicates that both girls and boys favor the male teachers. Thus the father may conduct these games for a brief period when he finishes his workday. If preschool children are worked with at home on some of these tasks, the middle and late mornings are probably best. The younger the child, the shorter the time spent on each game and on the total of the games. For example, if three- and four-year-olds can work for thirty minutes engaging in three games for ten minutes each, it would be fine. Much of the time their concentration span will not last that long, and a fifteen- or twenty-minute period involving two or three games will prove adequate.

Another good plan with the preschooler is to spend two days a week—for example, Tuesday and Thursday—with one kind of game, such as pattern recognition or serial memory, and to devote the Monday-Wednesday-Friday schedule to games involving letter recognition and/or number recognition. Lessons on all five days may be preceded with a few impulse-control activities to calm the children down and gain their attention.

Who and How Many?

Certain of these games can be played by children of all ages, of both sexes, and of varying degrees of intelligence. The games are followed by a statement about the general age and intelligence range for whom they are designed.

Much of my research has been conducted within the south-central area of Los Angeles, and my subjects have consisted of Negro and Mexican-American children from grades one through four. These games are also being employed in the schools of an affluent district in Los Angeles County.

Most of the schools for the physically and mentally handicapped in the city of Los Angeles have designed their playgrounds during the past five years to accommodate many of these games. Children in these schools, who have been classified as trainable mentally retarded, educable mentally retarded with physical disabilities, or intellectually capable but physically handicapped, have had varying degrees of exposure to these activities with apparent success. Some of the books in the Bibliography for this chapter contain activities specifically designed for physically handicapped youngsters.

These games, although they may prove to be fun, are less helpful as one ascends the intellectual and age scale. Bright children of eight and older who engage in classroom exercises in a well-motivated manner do the mental mechanics of reading, arithmetic, etc., far quicker than they can exercise their competencies by jumping into squares or running relays. Thus for these children playing various learning games may be a waste of time and facilities.

At the same time children in these older age groups who are not well motivated when seated in a classroom and yet who possess good intellects are likely to "blossom" when exposed to the prospect of combining fun and learning in one package. My fellow researchers, instructors, and I frequently encountered this type of child when conducting research in some of the less privileged areas of Los Angeles. Teachers observing these children have reported that their whole attitude toward learning had changed after engaging in these games—a change that was reflected in increased effort at school tasks no matter where they were taught or what subjects were involved. They liked the games, played hard, thought about them, and achieved success for the first time in their lives. This new feeling of success supported and undergirded their efforts when they attempted other more difficult tasks in less motivating surroundings.

Many older Negro boys in some schools within the central city of many large metropolitan areas are for many obvious and not so obvious reasons difficult to reach with traditional teaching practices. Although it is more than dangerous to attach absolutes to any statement about education and learning, I believe that many of these boys could not and cannot be reached with important verbal-reading skills *in any other way* than the game approach advocated in this book. The ability to read is virtually nonexistent in the hierarchy of values of some of these children. They are physically tough and—perhaps surprising to white educators—can often engage in flexible and descriptive verbal behavior. It *is* important to be able to "con" people in the ghetto, and to entertain oneself often requires the ability to exchange verbal barbs and jokes. However, it has been pointed out by more than one researcher on the subject that it is usual to find that culturally deprived children and youths place little value on reading. Often black, brown, or white ghetto youths neither know nor care whether their best friends read.

Action is important for these children. Many boys from father-absent homes assert their feelings of manhood, which are sometimes stifled in mother-dominated homes, in several ways. They play games and are in all ways interested in sports and in sports heroes. Secondly, they may cut off all things feminine, including the feminine teacher and most of the subjects she is trying to get across to them.[1]

One researcher has found that the only subject in elementary school felt to be masculine by boys is mathematics; the other subjects are viewed as passive and feminine. Thus it is believed that for boys who are presently in underprivileged areas, as for no other group, these games may offer one of the few ways they can be induced to participate actively in the learning process.

As is often true in education, the smaller the group, to a point, exposed to these games, the more improvement may be expected. Small groups permit more chances for a given child to do a given operation, and at the same time the observing teacher is more likely to be able to see what transpires and see the accuracy and quality of the children's responses.

In the research conducted on the games, the classes have at times ranged as large as twelve and fourteen. When working with these numbers, it is often possible to divide the group into effective smaller working "teams." These teams, at times composed of observers, problem givers, and problem solvers, can frequently rotate roles, and a good learning environment for all can be created. Many of the games can also be carried out by the twenty to forty or more usually found in the elementary school classrooms.

It could be argued that any more advantageous teacher-pupil ratio than is normally found in class would elicit improvement in the academic competencies of elementary and secondary school children. However, my research projects usually had small control groups in them who worked in the usual manner at desks. When their improvement scores were compared to the improvement of the small learning-games groups, the differences were more often in favor of the latter.

---

[1] This is not to imply that feminine teachers are necessarily bad for boys in schools. But the data suggest that boys' values in school and their methods of behaving are different from those of girls and that accommodation to these differences is important for the teacher to engage in, regardless of whether the teacher is male or female.

It has also been argued that it is too expensive to place children in groups smaller than the thirty-five to fifty sometimes found in elementary schools for any kind of special help. However, in pretests carried out at many schools in which we later inserted learning games, it was found that from 10 to 15 percent of the children tested in grades three and four (eight- and nine-year-olds) did not know all the letters of the alphabet. And yet these children had been passively (or actively) residing in these classes for three or more years, not learning very much of anything having to do with letters, spelling, reading, or other written and verbal communication skills. One wonders whether it is more expensive to turn out this percentage of functional illiterates or whether it might be less expensive to extend remedial tutoring help in the form of games or through some other devices during these early school years when it is needed. I vote for this latter course of action.

With What and Where?

It is suggested that various letter squares, number squares, lines, etc., are necessary to play the various games. Several manufacturers (listed in the Appendix) are presently making these letter squares, but I have made squares of this nature by cutting up rubber carpet matting and then stenciling letters with spray paint on their surfaces. Letters on Masonite squares may also be used; however, they make a clatter when jumped on and do not adhere to a floor or cement surface as the commercially produced letters, numbers, and rubber squares will do. If you use the Masonite letters, they may be placed in frames that hold them together and prevent them from slipping.

The lines indicated in several of the games may be made with Scotch tape #471, which is yellow, flexible, and about two inches wide. Lines, as well as letter and number grids, can be painted permanently on a playground. These grids should contain letters in squares about one foot square. There should be about thirty-six letters, six to a side in each grid. In this manner the squares are large enough to contain the child's heel, and adjacent squares containing letters or numbers needed to carry out a given game are also close enough to jump in.

Tape is probably best for various configurations. In this manner the problems can be changed rather frequently, and thus the children's interests can be maintained. The commercially produced letter, number, and geometric configuration squares are likely to be better than those you may make yourself.

Clinical investigations have shown that these games are effective if conducted at times in the classroom and at other times in multipurpose rooms, unused cafeterias, auditoriums, stages, and playgrounds. If the children are very young, it is sometimes not advisable to begin in too large a space until a reasonable amount of control can be exerted by the teacher and accepted by them. Often when less mature groups, or groups less capable intellectually, are led to a playground, they tend to scatter rather quickly, imposing difficult supervision problems.

At home the game room, driveway, or patio can also be used effectively by parents. Most of the materials are easily taken up and down and do not pose problems if these areas are used for other purposes at other times.

How to Teach

It is not my intention to describe a teaching philosophy or even a brief model for a methodology of education; others have carried out this assignment with more facility than I have. (Their references are listed at the end of this chapter for your later inspection.) There are, however, several principles important to using these learning games that my observations have proven to ensure maximum success and minimum chance of chaos.

1. To children, games are opportunities to be extremely active. During the initial stages of teaching these games, it may be necessary to exert more control than might be advisable later in the semester. Younger children in particular, it has been found, benefit greatly from a concentration on various impulse-control games and the like prior to being introduced to the more advanced games in which pattern, letter, and number discrimination is required.

After practice in these games, it may be necessary to engage in various forms of relaxation training. At other times relaxation training or some modification of it may have to be inserted between various learning games. Games of this nature, if they are not handled correctly, will sometimes overexcite hyperactive, distractible children.

2. In all cases, attempt to involve the children in the evaluation and planning of these activities. Many, if not most, of the games contain provisions for student involvement. It should be encouraged, taking into consideration their level of maturity and previous experience not only at making decisions but at taking part in games of this nature. Generally the progression for gradually releasing control to students when they are capable is as follows:

   a. Start with teacher-directed activities. Children copy and respond exactly to instructions from an adult. Modifications of the task are accepted only with the permission of the teacher.

   b. If the children are capable of following directions well, give them an opportunity to make minimal decisions concerning task modifications. For example, they might be asked to present their own problems on a blackboard, to which their fellow students can jump the answer. Or they may devise new ways to get from one point to another in a letter relay. The teacher in this second phase still retains most of the decisions herself, and the modifications can be only within a relatively narrow range of choice. Most important of all, she still retains the decisions about evaluation. It is still the teacher who states whether a child is correct or who gives some sign of approval when a job is well done.

   c. If it is found that the students respond well to making decisions about ways in which the tasks might be modified, they may then be given further decisions to make. For example, decisions about evaluation may be extended to them. Many of the games have provisions for student observers and correctors of the quality of peer responses. When the teacher appoints judges of this type, she should not suddenly take back this type of decision. She should then always ask the judge or evaluator how the performer is doing, rather than go directly to the performer to extend her criticism or encouragement. In this stage a great deal of student involvement of an intellectual nature will become apparent as all students become careful observers of the responses of their friends in the class.

d. A final stage may be reached when the children are simply given general instructions concerning goals and are then permitted to devise ways of teaching the goals within the general context of learning games. Children should not be given this type of global decision unless they have displayed their competencies and responsibilities in Steps b and c. But if they have, the teacher may, for example, suggest that the class could improve in spelling and ask what games they would suggest to effect this improvement. The children should be given time to engage in silent thought (just as they should in Steps b and c). A child thinking is a beautiful sight that some teachers may never have observed.

Any of the games may be played at these four levels of control. For example, games in pattern recognition may be carried out by asking the child to devise several ways of jumping into a circle after he finds it from among several figures; in this same game, observing children can count the number of responses and determine whether the performer really found the circle before jumping in it.

The other games can also be played under strict teacher direction or with more freedom extended if the children can handle it. The schema presented on these pages does not originate with me but has been expounded by Mosston and others during the years. However, it is not a "throw the doors open and let chaos take place" type of program. If it is found, for example, that the children cannot even take the responsibility for making minimal decisions about modifying the task, the teacher should take over direction again. However, there are several keys to encouraging children to make these kinds of helpful decisions about their educational program.

Give them time to think. Secondly, *be happy with whatever they come up with* (if it is safe). *It may be the only original thing they have ever been given the opportunity to devise that day or even that year in school! Remain relaxed and resist the temptation to show them your way of hopping in a square. The process of arriving at their own way is obviously more important than how they get in the square!*

I have observed wonderful responses from children with whom this approach has been employed. Perhaps if your own needs for authority permit, you may try this type of teaching also.

There are many other teaching guidelines that should be adhered to when employing these movement games. For example, it should *never* be assumed that the children know the reason for the game and will somehow, without your help, transfer what qualities are elicited in the game to classroom operations or to life. For example, when teaching impulse-control activities, tell the children why you are doing it. "Some of you have trouble sitting still in class. I hope that these kinds of games will help you realize that you can control yourself and you can relax and be happier sitting for longer periods of time in class. Let's see if they do!"

Or maybe, "I know that some of you are having trouble learning to spell, and I thought perhaps if we played an enjoyable game together that spelling might be more fun for you and that you will really improve. Shall we try?"

Or perhaps, "Johnny, you seem to have trouble remembering directions or the manner in which letters should be placed in words. Perhaps if we play this game together (a serial memory game), you may be helped to remember things better."

Or, "You are having trouble remembering the names of your letters. Perhaps if we start with a few simple figures like these and then see how they may be changed into letters, remembering letters might be easier for you."

Or finally, "Mike, I find that you do not read very well, and when watching you work in class I see that you do not seem to like to practice reading. I watched you in the playground the other day and saw how much you enjoyed playing games, so I thought that if we played some reading games together your reading might improve and the practice would be fun for you."

Although a strict behavioral scientist would blanche at these tactics (as without doubt they would result in "throwing the results of the experiment in the direction wished for by the experimenter"), it *is* believed that this type of teaching for transfer—of building "thought bridges" between activities—is sound applied educational psychology. Teachers and parents are not conducting experiments. They want maximum results from their efforts. By following some of these guidelines they may achieve the best results with the children participating.

Adjusting the Difficulty of Recognition Lessons

Three primary conditions contribute to the difficulty of learning to identify patterns, letters, and numbers. One revolves around the way the stimulus is presented. For example, the child learns most easily when the teacher names the letter (or other figure) and shows it at the same time. Learning is more difficult when the teacher just exposes the letter or figure to visual inspection before the child makes a verbal or a motor response (e.g., jumping into the correct square). The most difficult learning situation is when the word, letter, or number is merely named by the teacher, without any visual presentation of its conformations.

The number of discriminations a child must make at a time is a second factor affecting the difficulty of games within this general identification category. How many letters, numbers, etc. are present when he must select the correct one? The child standing in front of just one letter (or square) and looking, one at a time, at letters presented on the blackboard is learning at the easiest level. The next order of difficulty involves the selection, from two or three letters, of the one which is presented by the teacher or called out by her. The difficulty increases as the number of letters in front of the child is increased.

If a delay is required between the time the letter or other figure is shown and/or named and the time the child must respond in some way, this creates a third condition which makes the letter, number, and word recognition games increasingly difficult for the child. An immediate response by the child (e.g., jumping directly on the word or letter square) is easiest. Next in order of difficulty is a short wait. Most difficult for the child is a prolonged wait. Research has shown that, unless a number or a group of numbers or letters that is to be remembered is not mentally rehearsed within one minute of its presentation to the learner, forgetting is likely to occur and the information will not "drop" into a medium or long term memory storage bin. When introducing time delays, the teacher should aid a child to rehearse mentally and/or verbally what he is required to remember and to respond to later.

When presenting various games in which the purpose is to aid a child to recognize letters, numbers, geometric figures, and words, the teacher should keep these guidelines in mind. She should introduce difficulty by requiring more discriminations and by introducing a time delay between presentation and the response required. She should present the stimulus figure that is to be remembered in increasingly difficult ways (visual–verbal, visual only, or verbal only) when the children seem able to deal with more complexity. On the other hand, if she has trouble eliciting the proper responses from her charges, the teacher should also be ready to reduce the difficulty of her lessons by working backward within these three scales of difficulty.

Retention

The last subject we will cover in this methods chapter is remembering, or retention. There are a number of ways to achieve the greatest amount of retention, including telling children that they will be asked later to again perform some task they are practicing.

Overlearning also elicits maximum retention. If, for example, it is desired that all letters of the alphabet can be remembered one time perfectly, the children should practice the alphabet until they can say, write, and pronounce it two or three times in succession without mistake (200–300 percent overlearning in this case).

Movements or verbal information in rhythmical form is more likely to be retained than nonsense syllables or disconnected movements or words. This is why memory devices for verbal information are often learned in the form of poems. Music and rhythm connected to some of the games may enhance retention. An alphabet song, for example, may be helpful.

Summary

This chapter outlines basic principles relative to the application of the learning games. The spacing of practice, rewards for performance, and the sequence of activities are discussed.

Important suggestions for the degree of student involvement versus teacher domination are listed. For a more comprehensive look at this aspect of teaching, the reader is referred to the text by Mosston in the Bibliography for this chapter.

The principles of transfer are illustrated in several paragraphs. I also point out concrete ways to encourage a child to gain insight into the relationship between a learning game and classroom operations. The chapter concludes with suggestions for enhancing retention and adjusting difficulty.

Bibliography

BRUNER, J. S., *Toward a Theory of Instruction.* Cambridge, Mass.: The Belknap Press of Harvard University Press, 1966.

CRATTY, B. J., and SISTER M. M. MARTIN, *Perceptual-Motor Efficiency in Children.* Philadelphia: Lea & Febiger, Publishers, 1969.

ELLIS, H. C., *The Transfer of Learning.* New York: The Macmillan Company, Publishers, 1965.

MOSSTON, M., *Teaching Physical Education, From Command to Discovery.* Columbus, Ohio: Charles E. Merrill Books, Inc., 1966.

POPHAM, W. JAMES, and BAKER, EVA L., *Systematic Instruction,* Englewood Cliffs, New Jersey: Prentice-Hall, Inc., 1970.

Chapter 11

Improving Coordination

Chapter 1 contained a brief discussion of the problems the clumsy child faces in school, in his home, and while playing in his neighborhood. My research, as well as work at other laboratories in this country and abroad, suggests that it is possible to change the way children move by exposing them to various kinds of remedial tasks. This chapter outlines briefly some procedures to correct the movement problems of some children.

How Long Will It Take? What Changes? Who Changes?

Generally a child with coordination problems should be given some kind of extra help during most of his early elementary school years. Often this kind of special attention must be continued throughout his entire school career.

133

How Long Will It Take?
What Changes?
Who Changes?

The amount of change that can be expected in a given child is often difficult to predict. However, I have found that two factors influence just how much change may be forthcoming: the age of the child and the degree of impairment. Younger children improve more. Somehow the child's nervous system is more likely to change before the age of seven or eight. In one study I carried out, three times as much improvement was seen in children between the ages of four and seven than in those in late childhood. Although this marked difference stemmed partly from the characteristics of the test used, these findings do argue for the early identification and remediation of children with coordination problems. Furthermore, children with moderate or mild problems are more likely to be helped by corrective activities than are those with more severe problems.

Determining just what it is that changes when a child seems to become better able to use his body in various tasks is a difficult undertaking. Subtle neurological changes may result from participation in some kind of remedial program, which in turn results in an improvement in general coordination. However, practice of motor activities on the part of clumsy children may simply lead them to adopt better ways of performing and better performing strategies rather than to any basic adjustments in their neuromotor makeup. Even these types of positive changes in learning technique can be extremely helpful. Learning how to guide a pencil and how to hold the paper are examples of this "learning how to learn" that may result in increased clarity of handwriting. It may be equally helpful if a clumsy child with balance problems learns that he must stand with a slightly wider stance when throwing or in other ways must adjust his body to overcome or submerge his minor handicap when he is performing various tasks. The result is likely to be improvement, which may encourage him to try harder at other new movement activities.

Although it is clear that performance changes *do* take place on standard tests of movement competency, the mechanisms underlying these changes are less clear. A more thorough treatment of the question "What is it that changes?" may be found in a recent investigation in which I compared the pretest and posttest performances of clumsy children in a six-month program of remedial activities. These children came twice a week and spent one hour in small groups, engaging in various movement tasks under the supervision of an instructor. Four types of changes were evaluated, and at the same time their improvement was contrasted to that of a control group in a nearby school district (whose physical education program left much to be desired).

In general, rather dramatic changes occurred in tests of muscular fitness, including measures of arm, upper back, chest, lower back, and abdominal strength and endurance. Significant, but less marked, changes occurred in tests measuring agility, balance, ball throwing and catching, and the like. During this same interval, however, no significant changes were recorded in a test in which scores were based on how the children felt about their physical appearance and ability. It thus appeared that this type of feeling about oneself is not improved so quickly as some of the performances that contribute to this portion of a child's self-concept.

It is believed that the parents of a clumsy child should not despair but should be practical and take positive steps to aid their child to become more proficient with his body. At the same time school personnel should provide special classes in the regular elementary and secondary schools. Two or three times a week children with coordination problems should engage in remedial tasks to improve their abilities to play childhood games and to help them to write and to use their hands better in various equally necessary tasks.

Who Is Clumsy?

Clumsy children are identified in formal and informal ways. A child with severe movement problems usually elicits the concern of the obstetrician delivering him. At birth, flaccid hands, atypical birth reflexes, and/or unusual eye movements pinpoint the child with some kind of neurological problem of a rather marked nature.

More prevalent, however, are children whose coordination problems are not so obvious and may not manifest themselves until later in infancy. These children are usually first seen as having some kind of difficulty when they first try to use tableware, dress themselves, or learn to tie their shoes. They may seem to stumble a lot when learning to walk and are usually delayed in gaining these basic kinds of movement skills.

If the parents are concerned or affluent enough, they may, sometime during the first five years of the child's life, have a rather thorough neurological examination or some kind of a "work-up" of perceptual motor functioning carried out by a physician or psychologist. Often this type of minor but measurable coordination problem is accompanied by hyperactivity or unusually phlegmatic behavior. These same children are often delayed in learning the names of their body parts, particularly their left and right sides. They not only fumble their forks and spoons but also draw poorly, and on entering school they cannot keep up with their friends in the first letter-printing problems confronting them there.

There are several types of screening tests that may be administered to children of three, five, and seven years who are suspected of having some kind of problem. There are no well-established and comprehensive norms for evaluating the motor coordination of a large number of children of these ages; however, research has provided general guidelines that, if applied to young children, pinpoint those who not only need a more thorough "work-up" by a physician and psychologist but who, more importantly, should participate in some kind of remedial activities.[1]

By the age of three a child free from coordination problems should be able to:

1. Walk a line two inches wide on a floor for a distance of about ten feet without "falling off."
2. Hold a crayon and inscribe a simple cross if given a model to copy.
3. Walk with a rhythmic gait pattern, with the arms relaxed and moving in coordination with the feet (i.e., left arm advanced while left leg moves forward).

---

[1]A more comprehensive survey of expected levels of competency in a large number of movement tasks is contained in B. J. Cratty, *Perceptual and Motor Development of Infants and Children*, New York: The Macmillan Company, 1970.

4. Jump forward three times with both feet leaving the ground at the same time.
5. Run forward and walk backward without stumbling for short distances.
6. Name body parts and parts of the face, including the limbs, stomach, front, back, head, eyes, ears, nose, mouth, hands, and first and little fingers.

Generally, at this age, girls as a group will perform slightly better in these tasks than will boys.

By five years the girls will continue to excel the boys, but both boys and girls should be able to:

1. Draw circles and squares with reasonable accuracy. (At times they may not close their circles, or they may overlap the ends of lines forming both circles and squares.)
2. Jump, both feet at a time, over a stick about ten inches from the ground.
3. Touch, one at a time in order, each finger to the tip of the thumb of the same hand. This may be done slowly and with close attention by a child of this age.
4. Be aware of his left hand, leg, etc., although not necessarily of which side is which (he should be consistent in these judgments, however—i.e., placing the right leg on the same side, even if incorrect, as the right arm and ear).
5. Hop on one foot two or three times.
6. Balance, without moving, on one foot, with his eyes open for a period of from four to six seconds.
7. Get up from a back-lying position to his feet in about two seconds when asked to do so as fast as he can.
8. Print his first name using letters about one or two inches high (he may reverse some letters).

By the age of seven years a wider range of abilities should be evidenced. For example, at seven a child should be able to:

1. Draw a triangle with reasonable accuracy and print letters about a quarter of an inch high and level with one another. (He generally will not reverse letters at this age.)
2. Skip, alternating feet in a rhythmic manner.

3. Throw a ball using the proper mechanics (i.e., advancing the foot opposite to the throw and showing a proper weight shift forward as the ball is released).
4. Throw a playground ball about fifteen feet into a square target about four feet square.
5. Run vigorously using the proper arm action; jump upward or forward using the proper arm action at the same time (i.e., extending the arms upward and/or forward depending on what jump is being made).
6. Evidence little left-right confusion when asked to name body parts properly.
7. Touch each finger quickly and in order to the thumb of the same hand.
8. Skip and jump with accuracy into small squares one foot by one foot in size.

By the ages of nine and ten, children are able to catch small balls thrown from a distance and to play reasonably complex games, remembering the rules with little difficulty. By this age they should be able to write legibly and to copy three-dimensional figures (i.e., cubes, cylinders) with little difficulty. Their balance should enable them to posture on one foot with their eyes closed for a considerable period of time. Their strength should be increasing, and they should be able to do several situps and a pushup or two. If the children in your charge cannot carry out the above tasks at the ages indicated, there is some cause for concern. They should be evaluated more carefully by a physician or psychologist and should be exposed to some kind of remedial program designed to correct their deficiencies.

In the following two sections general principles as well as examples of remedial motor tasks will be outlined. For more thorough discussions of remedial activities, consult the Bibliography for this chapter.

Writing and Drawing Skills

As has been explained, by the time a child enters the first grade he should be able to draw reasonably accurate squares and circles and print his first name (although this latter task is usually carried out with some effort and not very capably).

If you inspect the writing and drawing attempts of your child carefully, you may see several types of problems that prevent him from doing well. He may, for example, evidence a slight tremor in his work; when trying to draw a straight line, it ends up looking like this:

A child with printing problems may also have difficulty stopping his movements when appropriate. For example, asked to connect two dots, he may overdraw them like this:

or perhaps "overshoot" the drawing of squares, circles, or letters like this:

At the same time the child may have difficulty copying figures, singly and in relation to one another. For example, when shown this,

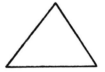

it may be written like this:

While trying to copy this,

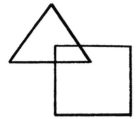

it might come out like this:

At other times a child's eye seems to move ahead or lag behind inappropriately as he draws lines and performs similar acts. Thus he will draw in periodic, sporadic movements, wait for his eyes to catch up or to come back to his hand, and then continue. Thus, instead of drawing a line from one dot to a second like this,

his efforts may take this form:

Another cause for poor writing and printing behavior may be a visual problem. He may appear to get too close to his work.

At other times children cannot write well because they cannot hold the writing implement efficiently. Still another problem preventing good written work is the inability to organize complex letter shapes and word shapes when attempting to copy them well. Thus, when shown this,

the child may actually see and thus draw this:

To determine whether writing and printing problems are caused by visual-perceptual difficulties or difficulties in hand-eye coordination during the writing act, it is sometimes helpful to ask a child if a figure he has drawn while looking at another figure is to him really the same or different. Thus when shown this,

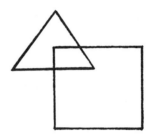

and after drawing this,

a child might say that indeed he sees them as both the same, in which case a visual perceptual problem is probable. Or he may say that he knows his is not so accurate as the one he was shown, which may indicate that he has difficulty moving his hand correctly.

Helping a Child to Write and Print Better

Helping a child to write and print better can be a stressful undertaking for the parent or teacher as well as for the child himself. Thus one of the first rules to follow is to make the practice as much fun as possible. Secondly, do not prolong the training for too long during a single practice period: about twenty minutes a day is maximum.

Prior to giving a child training in writing, it is helpful to do two things: (1) help him hold his writing implement correctly, and (2) help him determine, if it is not clear, just which hand works best for him.

The writing implement should be held in a relaxed manner between the thumb and the first two fingers. The wrist and arm should move in a relaxed manner, as should the fingers. The pen or pencil should be held firmly but not with too tight a grip. During the child's initial writing efforts, he should be shown how to hold the pen or pencil so that he will not start with an incorrect grip on the implement.

Deciding which hand a child prefers to write with can be an extremely puzzling task. At various times most children (as well as adults) use one hand for some tasks and the other hand for other tasks. One way in which clinical psychologists evaluate hand preference is to give a child five or six one-handed tasks that are reasonably difficult for that child. Simply asking him to pick up an object in front of him will not do the trick, as there is likely to be a 50–50 response with either hand. Rather, the tasks should be reasonably difficult and could include, for example, cutting with scissors, combing the hair, reaching into a tube to retrieve a piece of candy, drawing a triangle, etc. These tasks should be given three times a week, preferably for two or three weeks. Score should be kept concerning the hand preferences a child indicates for each task. The percentage of time the left versus the right hand is used on these tasks should be computed. Perhaps in this manner you will be able to see a general tendency in hand usage that will aid you to guide a child to the hand most helpful to him for writing. That the writing hand he chooses is not similar to his preferred eye is of little significance; likewise, it is no cause for concern if his foot preference does not match his hand preference.[2]

---

[2] Several texts listed in the Bibliography for this chapter contain highly detailed discussions of hand usage, cross dominance, and similar topics as related to educational functioning of children. The reader is urged to consult these references if additional information is desired on this highly complex subject.

It is important at this point for the child to know the *name* of the hand he habitually uses and to be able to tell when he is using the other hand for other purposes. Once the child's preferred writing hand is decided on and he evidences the ability to grasp the writing instrument correctly, then a decision should be made concerning the amount of guidance he needs to produce reasonably accurate figures, letters, and the like. He may be started at one of five stages of control. For example, if his movements are extremely erratic, the hand he writes with may have to be held by his parent or teacher while he moves his hand. The helper can hold the pencil, make a small block through his letters, or draw various geometric lines slanting laterally. At the same time he should be encouraged to watch these movements and to try to take over the guidance of his hand himself. Sometimes bright lining tape placed on a table and outlining these various figures and letters is helpful.

Generally when practicing these tasks, it is usual for a left-handed child to move clockwise around the various geometric figures and to start his squares and rectangles in the upper- right-hand corner and his triangles and circles at the top. The right-handed child usually starts his triangles and circles in the same spot but moves in a counterclockwise manner around these figures, as well as around squares and other figures, starting his rectangles and squares in the upper- left-hand corner.

If a child's inaccuracies are not so pronounced, he may be aided to control his writing and printing movements by various grooved surfaces through which he may trace geometric figures and block-printed letters. He should be encouraged to start these figures and to use his preferred hand, holding the writing implement correctly.

If this type of grooved writing and printing is accomplished with a minimum of guiding, retracing of movements, etc., the child may next be given templates to trace around. These instruments are slightly more difficult than the grooves, because they provide guidance on only one side of the figures, whereas the grooves provide guidance on both sides of the line being copied.

After a period of weeks, months, or even years, the child may be ready next to take over more control of his movements. One of the more successful ways to provide a transition between the grooved and template writing and printing and the more difficult task of tracing over various figures and copying figures without any guidance whatsoever is to employ shallow pans of modeling clay through which children can draw letters and figures.

Shallow clay, placed in a large cookie pan as shown, provides a bit of tension but at the same time gives the child some control over the implement. When writing in the clay, slight erratic movements are controlled. To provide an increasingly difficult task, the layer of clay can be reduced in thickness. When the clay becomes "torn up" through practice, it can be placed in the oven and melted again.

The next step in aiding a child to gain control of his hand movements in printing and writing consists of requiring him to draw various figures, letters, etc., with the use of various visual guideposts. For example, he may be asked to draw between lines placed decreasing widths apart and of increasing complexity as shown.

Dots may be connected as an exercise within this general practice level. These dots may encourage a child to move accurately throughout his space field as shown.

Later the dots may be arranged so that connecting them will result in various block-printed letters as shown.

The final stage of eliciting control of handwriting movements involves letting the child draw his own letters without guidance, and with or without guiding lines to keep the letters even. These exercises are commonly used during the first two or three years of elementary school; if the child is not capable of executing his numbers and letters within this relatively unstructured situation by the time he is six or seven, he is likely to have a difficult time performing up to expectations in school.

Remember that these exercises should be made fun. Geometric figures may be made into people and houses; letters may form words that describe pictures a child has drawn. Several brief sessions each day are better than one long and taxing one.

My research has indicated, despite some popular opinion to the contrary, that improvement in this type of task may be elicited only by practice specifically in these activities. No magic transfer to writing accuracy will occur from activities involving large-muscle control (i.e., balance agility, etc.). Measurable, and at times remarkable, change will occur in a child's hand-eye coordination, manifesting itself in increased proficiency in writing and printing tasks, if the principles and exercises described here are employed. If a child in middle and late childhood continues to evidence pronounced problems in writing, it may be helpful to teach him the typewriter keyboard. Often children are more skilled in this type of aiming task with the finger (i.e., typing) than they are at writing. Thus typing provides an outlet for the intellect that may be blocked when the child tries to write out his ideas on paper.

Control of the Larger Muscles

Exercises in improving activities requiring the larger muscles of the body can also lead to improvement of various performance tasks. I studied a group of children exposed to some of the activities outlined below for two one-hour sessions per week for five months. Contrasted to a control group who received no type of remediation, the experimental group showed significant changes.

Some of the best indices of problems in big-muscle control are the balance tasks outlined previously in this chapter.

At the same time there are several types of big-muscle activities to which the clumsy child should be exposed, including balance, agility, jumping, hopping, and the like, as well as tumbling movements and ball throwing and catching.

Clumsy children evidence several general types of movement problems when asked to show control of their larger muscles. They often cannot vary the speed with which they move and are unable to stop movements when appropriate. Just as was mentioned in the section dealing with writing, there seems to be one "force" output to their movement computer. They are likely to throw a ball too hard to an individual standing close to them and will have difficulty running and then stopping quickly when attempting to retrieve a ball thrown to them.

Secondly, they have trouble integrating movements in various parts of the body. They do not lift their hands and arms upward as they extend their legs in jumping upward. They do not shift their weight and step correctly when they throw a ball. Thus they do not jump with their arms and throw with their legs as do many children.

These difficulties may come about partly because of a lack of opportunity to participate. These children may have withdrawn from competition, thus compounding their problems, when they have discovered their ineptitude in games. Also, some of these children, perhaps beset with visual-perceptual problems, may not have been able to see and to copy the efficient movements of their playmates. Thus they may be unable to see and to imitate appropriate running patterns, throwing movements, and similar basic activities.

There are several basic principles to follow when attempting to improve the abilities of children in tasks involving control of the large muscles.

1. Do not get stuck on one or two pet coordination exercises. To improve balance, a number of balance exercises should be employed. Walking lines, walking wide balance beams, and various standing and even seated balances should be engaged in. To improve running control, the children should be required to run in all directions, in various ways, and to stop and start in various ways.

2. Do not try to improve ball skills immediately by throwing balls at a child who cannot catch them very well. Start with such activities as foot soccer, jumping over lines, running backward, etc. to first give him an ability to move his body *to* a ball. Then, when picking up a ball, first try rolling it to him or teeing it up on a batting tee to hit it with a bat (even use a volleyball for hitting at first) before asking the child to catch a smaller ball coming from a considerable distance. Research indicates that this latter task is not well executed until children are about nine or ten years of age.

3. Teach children in middle childhood the specific game skills they need to "get by" in the games they are confronted with. Have them engage in the more basic agility and balance tasks they also need. Younger children can better confine themselves to the more basic activities, leaving complicated games skills to a later time.

4. Leave fitness exercises to the end of the practice period. Do not tire children out with programs of exercise at the beginning of the period. Save this time for agility activities, balance-beam walking, and the like.

5. For each lesson a child should be slightly overextended. Just as it is necessary to work hard in an exercise program to really get strength and/or endurance, it is also necessary to make a balance drill a little harder than the child would choose to impose upon himself. Make him hold a position a little longer than he could the day before and jump and hop with a little more accuracy and perhaps for a longer period of time than he would choose to do.

6. Make practice in big-muscle activities well motivated. Keep the child relaxed; abuse is not the way to make a child with coordination problems do better. The tension that ridicule will, and probably has, elicited in his life will contribute to his coordination problem.

7. Most important when working with a clumsy child is to try to "peel back" your sophistication. Do simple things with him—things he has trouble doing. See if he can jump over lines, jump down from low obstacles, run and stop, etc.

8. Finally, and most important, attempt when possible to involve the child intellectually in the movement tasks you undertake. He will think of many more ways to execute the various types of movements introduced to him. Practice of innumerable ways of accomplishing these various tasks will have a more marked effect than

simply copying a few stilted activities emanating solely from a teacher.

If these general guidelines are followed, a marked improvement will be seen in children to whom the following activities are introduced. The texts in the Bibliography for this chapter contain even more ideas.

Game 108
Jumping
Things

A child may be encouraged to jump and to hop in various ways over lines, ropes placed in a random fashion on the ground, hoops scattered around a field, or sticks placed in a variety of ways. By using different implements every few days, the tasks will remain new and interesting. Children may be asked to invent new ways to move around a course of this nature. Other games might include follow the leader, etc.

Falling frontward and backward, bending the knees and distributing the weight on the arms and legs while falling, and getting up and down in various ways aid a child to move efficiently in a vertical plane. Later the activities can lead to elementary rolling, and then simple tumbling tasks can be practiced.

It is fun to tumble and to roll down hills or down a mat, one side of which has been raised.

**Game 109
Tumbling
Things**

Obstacle courses can be made by placing two-by-fours on the ground. They can be made more difficult for more advanced children by placing things on the beams to walk over or by placing the beams so that the child must walk uphill or downhill on them. Brackets at the end can enable you to place the two-by-fours so that the two-inch edge must be walked on.

**Game 110
Balance
Things**

**Game 111
Throwing,
Catching,
and
Hitting
Balls**

The weight shift can be taught in throwing by having the child stand on a tilting platform that tips forward when the weight shift is made as the ball is released from his hand.

Children having trouble hitting balls can start by "golfing" a volleyball from the ground with a bat. It makes a satisfying noise when struck, and missing it is difficult because of its size. Later the ball can be rolled or bounced to the child. It can also be hit off a tee, and if these exercises are accomplished, balls of decreasing size can be used.

A child having difficulty catching a ball can have one rolled to him on the ground or down a groove. If a ball on a string is placed in various positions around him, he can anticipate its direction and predict its movement.

Throwing at targets of decreasing size placed on the ground and on walls can also improve throwing ability.

These and similar activities can improve the attributes inherent in the tasks. Improved fitness can be achieved by specific exercises to strengthen the shoulder region, the abdominals, and the lower back, as shown.

Chins can be performed as shown, keeping the feet on the ground, with a bar placed chest high. Younger children can thus perform from 4-8 of these, whereas with a higher bar they could not. This exercise tightens up the upper back muscles, improving posture.

For younger children, "knee pushups" can be performed, keeping the back straight. This exercise develops chest and upper arm muscles.

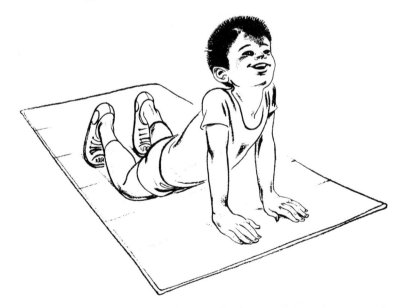

This should be done slowly, alternately raising the chest from the mat, and then lowering it to the mat. Feet may be held as shown to improve back strength.

Sit ups can be done as shown, with hands behind head, if the child is fit; or by reaching forward if the child is less fit. Feet may need to be held.

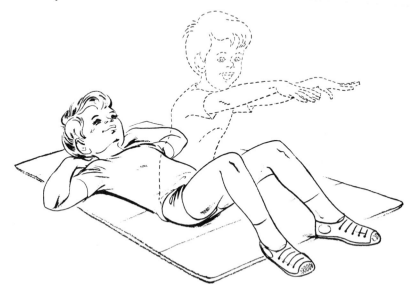

Keep improvement records in these exercises to aid motivation. Your session may terminate with these exercises, but following them you may want to try some of the impulse-control activities outlined in Chapter 2.

Coordination is complex. As you work with your children, you will find some who draw well but cannot balance and otherwise work in games. Some may be able to handle balls but cannot run well, and others will be poor in a number of types of tasks. With some experience, it should be possible to design programs of activities that will specifically meet the needs of individual children.

Providing a clumsy child with positive and concrete help in the form of these activities is important. In research carried out in 1966, it was found that children with coordination problems, as a result of apparently withdrawing from physical activity by late childhood, evidenced a shocking decline in physical abilities during these years and into late adolescence.

Children without movement problems become increasingly capable through adolescence. On the other hand, failure in physical activities elicits withdrawal and lack of participation, which in turn leads to a loss of capacity to perform. At the same time the development of increased abilities should and does have the opposite effect. It is hoped that the activities outlined in this chapter will reverse the failure, lack of participation, and lowering of capacities cycle that we often observe in the clumsy child.

Summary

This final chapter deals with methods through which children with coordination problems may be aided to move better. The two main sections contain activities for the improvement of fine motor control in writing and for enhancing large-muscle control, balance, and agility.

The earlier such remedial activities are begun, the more likely there is to be improvement. Likewise, children with mild to moderate problems are more likely to be helped than are those with more severe lack of coordination.

The chapter contains the results of recent research on this topic, together with principles for the application of motor training to children of various ages. Guidelines for the evaluation of the motor competencies of five-, seven-, and nine-year-olds are also provided.

Bibliography

CRATTY, B. J., *Developmental Games for Physically Handicapped Children*. Palo Alto, Calif.: Peek Publications, 1969.

———, *Trampoline Activities for Atypical Children*. Palo Alto, Calif.: Peek Publications, 1969.

CRATTY, B. J., and SISTER M. M. MARTIN, *Perceptual-Motor Efficiency in Children*. Philadelphia: Lea & Febiger, Publishers, 1969.

MOSSTON, M., *Developmental Movement*. Columbus, Ohio: Charles E. Merrill Books, Inc., 1965.

Equipment

1. The squares containing letters, numbers, and geometric figures mentioned in the descriptions of many of the games may be obtained from Action Learning, Inc., PO Box 49672, Los Angeles, Calif. 90049.

2. Lining tape may be obtained from hardware stores, and Scotch tape #471 may be used to produce the lines mentioned in many of the games.

3. Equipment produced by the Port-a-Pit Company, in Anaheim, California, may be used to produce the obstacle courses outlined in some of the games.

4. Prewriting Perceptual-Motor Exercises (recognition, recall, and reproduction). Teaching Resources, 100 Boylston Street, Boston, Mass. 02116.